ABOUT THE AUTHOR

After entering the profession 'by default', Steve Smith worked his way up from office boy's assistant ('my first job was to blow up a rugby ball for the senior partner's son') to co-founder of the criminal law practice Wilford Smith, based in Rotherham in South Yorkshire.

Junkies, Judges & Jail is the second in the comic legal series, following *Boozers, Ballcocks & Bail*.

A professional public speaker, Steve is married with a daughter and lives in Rotherham. He was awarded an MBE in the 2006 Queen's Birthday Honours List for his services to charity, and is president of Rotherham Town Cricket Club.

For further information about Steve Smith, visit his website at www.steve-d-smith.co.uk.

JUNKIES, JUDGES & JAIL

Stephen D. Smith

Neville Douglas Publishing Ltd

Published in 2007 by Neville Douglas Publishing Ltd, Barnsley, South Yorkshire, S73 0LY

Represented by Signature Book Services

10 9 8 7 6 5 4 3 2 1

A CIP catalogue record for this book is available from the British Library

Printed and bound in Great Britain by LPPS Ltd

ISBN-10 1-901853-72-1
ISBN-13 978-1-901853-72-8

Visit Steve Smith at www.steve-d-smith.co.uk

CONTENTS

To Jennifer and Rebecca with love

FOREWORD

There are certain people who have added immeasurably to the quality of my life: loving parents, my wife Christine and my four children, teachers with shining eyes, my editor at Penguin, and many more. And then there are writers like Steve Smith, who has delighted and entertained me with his stories of life as a criminal lawyer in a northern industrial town.

At a time when the publishing world is flooded with misery memoirs, it is refreshing to find books which lift the spirit and make the reader laugh out loud. And it is important to have books which make us laugh out loud, for laughter, the psychologists tell us, is good for us: increases our immunity to illness, improves sleep and enhances our lives. Steve Smith's books certainly do.

These aren't merely collections of funny tales: there is depth and quality to the writing. Here is an author who had blended hilarious anecdote with the most poignant and sometimes quite heart-rending descriptions of life on the wrong side of the law. He has peopled his vividly realised books with a rich tapestry of compelling characters — the incompetent, the foolish, the pathetic, the cruel, the vulnerable and the downright bizarre – all of whom are brought to life in richly comic and sometimes tragic situations.

Gervase Phinn

ACKNOWLEDGEMENTS

My thanks to everyone who has helped me with this undertaking, in particular my long-suffering family Jennifer and Rebecca.

Special thanks to Susanne McDadd for her support and the confidence she has given me to soldier on; her advice and guidance have been inspirational.

Cathy Douglas turned my manuscript into English with loving care and we had a lot of laughs along the way. Thank you also to Nancy Duin for her meticulous attention to detail.

My friends have encouraged me with advice and copious amounts of gin, which has kept us all entertained. Special thanks to Darren Millington, Colin Walker and Michael Smallwood.

I would also like to thank the following:

Ernest Booth Trio	Keith Gleeson
Central Books	Christopher 'Goody' Good
Neil Crossland	Jack Heptonstall
Cathy Douglas	Michael Jarvis
Mel Dyke	David 'Bader' Lister
Bob and Lynne Ego	Don Morton
(Sellars Restaurant)	Sean 'Pagey' Page
Brian Elliott	Lionel Parker
Michelle Fisher	Gervase and Christine Phinn
Fred the emphysemic	Signature
usher	Jennifer M Smith
Gillian Furniss	Rebecca E Smith
Tom 'The Hemingfield	And of course...
Fusilier' Furniss	Albert!

I also want to thank those lovely people who have visited the website and have contacted me with their views and good wishes. Since *Boozers*, I have had the opportunity of appearing at a number of literary festivals and met so many supporters that it has given me the confidence to release this, my second book in the series.

I hope they all approve.

PREFACE

It is the late 1980s. The Lord Chancellor's office had started to ruin the legal profession and the writing was on the wall for the Legal Aid Practitioner. I suppose we should have seen it coming but there were more immediate worries to contemplate and deal with.

The Heptonstall family upon whose patronage I had built the criminal law department of Wilford Smith & Co were flourishing but for them too the future had much in store.

I was enjoying life, with my new-found independence as a self-employed person at the forefront of my mind. I was fighting battles for those whose causes I felt were genuine and the business was growing, as were the members of staff, the overdraft and my waistline.

I had a brand spanking new BM. I cleaned it every day and wouldn't take it out in the rain. How I loved my Blue Metro!

I was entering into a new phase in my career. This is where my story continues...

ONE

ALL HE WANTS FOR XMAS IS A BOA CONSTRICTOR

'Tha sees, Steve, it's like this. Tha'll nivver believe it...'

It was almost 5.30pm on Christmas Eve 1982, and I was locking up Wilford Smith & Co, Solicitors of Rotherham on the wreckage of our Christmas party, when Albert Heptonstall appeared on my doorstep.

Albert was the youngest of Jack and Madge Heptonstall's nine children, whose family had been regular clients since I set up in business with my partner Steve Wilford in 1981. In fact he was the only one I hadn't yet represented in court, as he was only eleven, but there was plenty of time for him to follow the family tradition. Albert had already managed to break into a police compound, get into a police car and play with the short-wave radio, causing the complete breakdown of all the mobile police radios in the Rotherham area – not to mention trying to kill my tropical fish.

In the past, Albert had only ever come to the office with his father, but this time he was alone and looked unusually vulnerable, an undersized scruff minus the usual Heptonstall grin. I was about to learn that this wasn't all that had disappeared.

'We've lost Elliott,' said the usually happy-go-lucky lad tragically, his head bowed. 'He's gone.'

My mind raced through the names of Jack's children. Horace, Boris, Morris and Venn, Cloris, Doris, Lorris and Tyrone... But who the hell was Elliott? I could stand the suspense no longer. 'Albert,' I ventured, 'who's Elliott?'

'Me boa,' said Albert.

'Your what?' I asked, confused.

'Me boa,' said Albert.

I didn't want to show my ignorance, but there seemed no option. 'What's a boa?' I asked.

Albert paused for a moment, as if in a trance, then said, 'A constricting non-venomous reptile which crushes its prey by compression. The initial attack is remarkably quick, and usually made with the mouth open.' He demonstrated by forcing his mouth as wide open as possible, then continued: 'A coil is simultaneously thrown around the victim, and is then strengthened by other coils.'

Speechless, I felt my mouth drop further open than any boa constrictor's. How on earth could Albert speak so fluently and knowledgeably on such a subject?

He took my silence and surprised expression as a signal for further explanation. 'It's a snake, a bloody big'un an' all, five foot of 'im. Some git's pinched 'im, the thieving bastard,' Albert finished, and I finally understood.

I tried to cheer him up by asking: 'Where's the snake from, Albert?'

He brightened. 'South America, where the Indians come from. Tha knows Indians, dun't tha? Gandhi, Sitting Bull, Geronimo, tha knows?'

'Oh yes, of course,' I replied. I had difficulty with Albert's geography – in fact I had difficulty with just about everything Albert said – but at least on this occasion he seemed to mean well. 'How're your mum and dad, then, Albert?' I asked, to change the subject.

'Dad's aw reet, but Mum's upset. Tha'll nivver believe this neither, but we wa' burgled yisterday.'

'Never!' I said in astonishment.

'Aye,' said Albert. 'We were all aht, an' someone must have been watching t'ouse, 'cos they brock into my dad's shed and 'ad some of 'is tools away. They got inta kitchen an' all, and that's what really upset me muther. She'd a big pot o' stew on t'cooker like, ready to cook for tea. It must 'ave been some bugger wi' a grudge, 'cos the dirty bastard did 'is business in t'pot. It reet upset me muther, that did.'

'I can imagine, Albert. That's terrible,' I said, horrified.

'Aye,' said Albert. 'She was reet upset. She 'ad to chuck 'alf of it away.'

Only half of it? My mind boggled, and I quickly changed the subject again. 'What the hell were you doing with a five-foot boa constrictor in the first place, Albert?'

'Bugger all, now,' replied Albert in his eloquent way. ''E's gone, nicked, pinched, leafed, swiped, knocked off...'

I interrupted before he could think of more synonyms for the word stolen. 'How do you know he's been pinched?' I asked. 'Maybe he just slithered off.'

''E was in transit,' said Albert. He always phrased his replies in such a way as to keep the listener interested, almost as if he was sharing a secret with you, a trait he'd picked up from his father.

'In transit? From where and to where?' I asked.

'No – 'e was in t'Transit van!'

'Oh! So where's the van now?' I enquired cautiously.

'That's the point,' Albert whispered. 'It's gone an' all. Argh, nicked, pinched, leafed...'

'Yes,' I said, interrupting his flow. 'Now let me see if I've got this right. You have an extremely large snake which you keep in your father's van?'

'No,' Albert corrected me. 'Our Morris's van. You see, me father wain't let him in t'house, cos o' shit,' said Albert bluntly. 'Me father dun't like snake shit in t'house.'

'I can understand that,' I said, imagining what boa constrictor excrement might look like.

'Not only that,' continued Albert. ''E's a bit friendly, Elliott. We keep 'im in t'green'ouse, where it's warm, because 'e dun't like cold, tha sees. If we dun't ger'im back quick, 'e'll dee.'

I glanced out of the window at the Christmas tree in the church-yard, with its fairy lights on branches weighted with snow, then my thoughts returned to Albert, who had been concerned enough to walk the three miles from his home to my office in search of his bloody snake. I couldn't help thinking that there were plenty of snakes in Rotherham, not all of them reptiles.

'What do you feed him on?' I asked.

'Nowt, now,' said Albert sulkily.

'Before he was stolen, I mean,' I clarified.

'Oh, then?' said Albert. 'He'd eat the odd rat or mouse, or even summat bigger.'

'And how often did you have to feed him?' I asked.

'Ivvery day,' said Albert. 'If you don't, 'e gets restless, and that's when 'e gets a bit friendly round tha neck.'

'And then what does he do?' I asked.

'Squeezes,' answered Albert, making a gurgling noise.

'How long have you had Elliott?' I went on.

'About six months,' said Albert. 'I swapped him for three koi carp, a whippet, and some spare parts off me Dad's Skoda. It was a good deal really, because the Skoda's knackered and the whippet weren't in t'club, but it's gone to a reet good 'ome with a bloke who breeds them on a farm.'

'What was Elliott doing in the van?' I persevered.

''Avin' a change of scene. 'E was in his golf bag, where 'e lives. It's a big golf bag, and it opens at t'side instead o' t'top, and it's got, like, a cushion inside to keep him warm. He sleeps a lot, but he's reet affectionate.'

'Yes, I'm sure he is, particularly if he gets you round the neck. But aren't these types of snakes dangerous, Albert?' I asked.

'Nay, tha's just got to mek sure it dun't get thee round t'neck, or it'll gi' thee a reet 'eadache.'

It suddenly occurred to me that whoever had stolen the Transit van was driving around with a potentially lethal snake on board. Even if I wasn't worried about the thief's well-being, I certainly should be bothered about other road-users: if the snake got friendly while the driver was at the wheel, the consequences could be tragic. Besides, Albert wanted his snake back, and I imagined Morris also wanted his van. I began taking notes.

'What else was in the van?' I asked.

'There's an electric pump for a garden pond, and some spanners, and a big plastic doll, one o' them that blows up – our Morris borrowed it from Boris. Argh, and twenty thousand Benson and Hedges,' said Albert casually. 'They're mi Dad's, and 'e dun't know they've gone yet. 'E likes a smoke, tha knows. The thieving bastard will gerrit when me Dad finds aht,' Albert said, pulling a gruesome face and thumping his right fist into the palm of his left hand.

'I've no doubt, Albert,' I said. 'But that doesn't help the situation at the moment, does it?'

'What do I do, Steve?' asked Albert. 'It's Christmas, and I've got Elliott two rats for his present.'

I suggested that he report the theft to the police. 'Eh, I can't do that,' said Albert, 'Me Dad'll nivver wear that.'

'Fine, then I'll report it,' I replied. Albert was even less enthusiastic about this, but I reiterated my concerns for other road-users until he saw the point.

After a long discussion, we decided on our strategy. Albert would put an advertisement in the 'Lost and Found' section of the *Rotherham Advertiser*, in the hope that the thief or his associates might see it and feel disposed to hand back the stolen goods. I doubted whether this would achieve anything, but at least it was something to do. More importantly, it was Christmas Eve and the sooner we reached a decision, the sooner I would get home.

'Steve, would you write the advert for me?'

'Of course. I'll do it now, and you can add anything you feel appropriate,' I said. I took a piece of paper from the reception desk and wrote:

LOST OR STOLEN, ONE BOA CONSTRICTOR. A FORD TRANSIT VAN TAKEN ON 23RD DECEMBER CONTAINED A VERY DANGEROUS SNAKE, WHICH SHOULD BE RETURNED TO ITS OWNER IMMEDIATELY. PLEASE TELEPHONE 382121 AND ASK FOR ALBERT.

I handed the note to Albert, who felt he should offer something in return. 'Tha dun't want any bottles of whisky for Christmas, does tha, Steve?'

'No, thank you, Albert, I'm trying to give it up,' I answered, avoiding the prospect of handling stolen goods.

He got up from his chair and held out his hand for me to shake. I did so in the certain knowledge that the lad was destined to become a professional thief. Yet I couldn't help liking the little bugger – and Albert's behaviour wasn't all his own fault. Jack, his father, had never claimed benefit, but had lived a life of dishonesty, which his children accepted as normal. Albert had never been corrected or given proper direction, although he had been taught a certain moral code – he was respectful to the elderly and, like his father, would never consider defiling anyone's home by burgling it, although as Jack used to say, the 'commercials' were fair game.

At the door, Albert looked back at me in such a distraught way that I couldn't help feeling sorry for him. 'I will get 'im back, wain't I?' he asked pathetically.

'I hope so,' I replied. 'I really do.'

'Well, Merry Christmas then,' Albert said, trying to smile.

'Yes, Merry Christmas, Albert, and a Happy New Year.'

As I watched Albert trudge through the slush, I felt the cold wind blowing flecks of snow onto my face, shivered, and realised that Albert, in a greying T-shirt stained with gravy, under a National Coal Board donkey jacket with 'SECURITY' emblazoned on the back, wasn't dressed for a long walk home. I called him back, grabbed my coat and briefcase, and walked over to the taxi rank with him.

There were two taxis waiting, and I asked the driver of the first to deliver Albert to his front door. I paid, Albert jumped in, and waved as the taxi pulled off, the Heptonstall grin back on his face. At least the thought of arriving home in a taxi had made him forget Elliott for a moment.

I arrived home damp and nearly an hour late for our Christmas Eve dinner with the the Great Jarvis – our long-suffering accountant – and 'Tenbelly' Norburn and their partners (a tradition which continues today). My wife Jennifer was sitting in the hall dressed to the nines and tapping her foot vigorously; I'm afraid she wasn't impressed.

The phone rang early on Boxing Day. It was Rotherham police station, informing me that there was to be a special Boxing Day court, and my services had been requested by Eric Dobkin, alcoholic and reveller supreme, currently recovering in the local cells. He wanted me to represent him, but more importantly he was desperate for a packet of Benson and Hedges, as he had been without smokes all night.

Apparently, on Christmas night Eric had seen fit to climb the thirty-foot Christmas tree which was a feature of Rotherham's town-centre decorations. Having climbed up, he couldn't get back down, and eventually his weight made the tree topple, tipping him into the nearby fountain. This greatly entertained the gathered throng, but the officers of the South Yorkshire Police on duty were not amused, and arrested him for breach of the peace and criminal damage.

So, resigned to missing one of my favourite films – *The Prisoner of Zenda* starring Ronald Colman – I set off for the special lock-up court to see Eric, who wanted to make a formal complaint. He said the police had been visiting his cell in the early hours and deliberately keeping him awake by singing 'Silent Night'. I told him to concentrate on trying to get bail, but, as ever, Eric didn't agree with my advice. I hadn't been able to get him any cigarettes, but had found an old Christmas cigar, which I gave him. He smoked it furiously in the small interview room, making me splutter.

'Bad cough, that,' said Eric.

'Yes, it's the cigar smoke in such a confined space that's making me cough,' said I, hoping that he might put it out.

'That's a bugger, that,' sympathised Eric, continuing to puff away.

I managed to agree bail for Eric, on condition that he would not enter licensed premises. This didn't meet his approval either. 'What am I going to do about going out for a drink?' he asked. 'They can't stop me drinking in the house, can they?'

'No, so drink in the house then,' I replied.

'Neow, I'm not having that! Bloody hell, it's Christmas, for Christ's sake.'

I found this biblical utterance intriguing, but the magistrates had made their decision, and the boozers were out of bounds whether he liked it or not. The case was adjourned until the New Year, and I warned Eric that if he got arrested on New Year's Eve, no way would I turn out to help him.

I arrived home just as Ronald Colman was riding his horse into the sunset, being waved off by C Aubrey Smith and David Niven.

The next day, an advertisement in the local paper caught my eye. Under 'Lost and Found', I read:

NICKED WITH TRANSIT VAN, ONE BOA CONSTRICTOR (A SNAKE). THERE IS A REWARD FOR THIS VAN AND

CONTENTS AND THE BOA WHICH WERE STOLEN ON THE 23RD DECEMBER. REWARD OFFERED.

CAUTION WITH THE SNAKE, IT GETS FRIENDLY – PLEASE KEEP IT AWAY FROM NECK. IT ANSWERS TO THE NAME ELLIOTT. PLEASE RING JACK OR ALBERT ON ROTHERHAM 382121 OR WILFORD SMITH ON ROTHERHAM 828044.

That wasn't quite as I'd drafted it – I certainly didn't remember offering our office as a contact point to the 30,000 or so homes on the circulation list. I waited with bated breath to see what calls might come our way, and soon they did.

One caller wanted details of the thief so that he could 'kill him'. Another telephoned to say that he could give us no information at all, and a third offered to buy the snake if we found it. I told my omniscient and invariably competent secretary Sheila to refer the other callers to Albert, who wallowed in waves of sympathy from pet-lovers throughout South Yorkshire. The only thing we didn't receive was any information on Elliott's whereabouts.

On New Year's Eve, we were to close the office at noon. Unfortunately, at 9.15 am I received a telephone call requesting my attendance at the cells, to represent a local car thief who had committed offences while on bail.

Gerald David Robert Guthrie, known as 'Tank', was a lad of about twenty who had been brought up on a crime-ridden local housing estate, and had spent most of his short adult life in one custodial setting after another. There he enlivened the drudgery of institutional life by learning such essential skills as how to remove lead from roofs, hot-wire cars, and break windows silently with brown paper and treacle. Young Guthrie was almost as wide as he was tall, standing at five-foot-six but weighing eighteen stone; he once explained his obesity by telling me that it was achieved by being 'a pig'. His clothes were frayed, and looked as if he had out-

JUNKIES, JUDGES AND JAIL

grown them while wearing them, and his personal hygiene left a great deal to be desired, but he was easy to deal with. His speciality was car crime, which meant he stole either cars or their contents; it was said that he could beat any of the sophisticated electronic locking systems.

Tank came into the small interview room and I greeted him enthusiastically. 'Good morning, Mr Guthrie, and to what do we owe this pleasure? Don't tell me it's pinching cars.'

'Argh, Mr Smith, it is aye. I've got four charges and fifteen TICs [offences to be 'taken into consideration'], and don't tell me that I'm up shit creek for bail.'

Tank's forté was Fords, and true to form his four charges involved Cortinas, which he described as 'easy meat'. I didn't pay much attention to the list of offences to be 'taken into consideration', save to note that they were also Fords which Tank had freely admitted to stealing. 'Correct in all particulars, Mr Guthrie,' I said, 'and by the way, I love the suit.'

He was wearing a police-issue jumpsuit made out of a white paper-like material which covers the entire body, including the feet, and zips at the neck. They issue this snazzy item when they take a defendant's clothing for forensic tests. Tank was a suspect in a burglary in which threads from a jumper had been found on a broken window, and his clothing had been taken to see if the fibres matched. It was hot and stuffy in the tiny interview area, and before we headed for the court Tank unzipped the top of the jump-suit, to reveal not just his gold medallion but also some strange marks like tyre treads around his neck. As we walked up the spiral staircase to the courtroom I looked more closely, and noticed that the marks continued the full length of his neck.

I made the bail application as best I could but, not surprisingly, the magistrates were against me and remanded Tank in the local cells for three days while the police made enquiries into the burglary.

Court business over for the day, I returned to the office to catch up on things. As I came in, I gave a fond pat to the brass plaque we'd brought with us from Moorgate Street – the one my father had surreptitiously wept with pride over when we first mounted it. I said hello to Tracy as I passed through reception, and to Sheila at her desk outside my own office upstairs – where I found a large golf bag at the side of my desk, with a message attached:

> On seeing the advert in the paper, we realised this might be what you are looking for. Please return it to the owner.

There was no name or address, just the bag. I tentatively pulled open the zip and peered in cautiously, but found, to my horror, that the side zip was open and the bag empty.

For once, Sheila couldn't help. 'The bag was left in reception; Tracy didn't see who by,' she said. So I went in search of a snake, and in the corridor met Roy Bennett, our distinguished managing clerk, who at seventy still bore himself like a sergeant-major.

'Hello, Steve, are you looking for something?' he asked.

'Yes,' I replied, 'A snake.'

'Oh, he's in Wilf's room,' said Roy. 'You do mean Sean Page, don't you?'

The Honourable Sean Page, better known as Pagey, was a great friend but something of a menace at times. 'No,' I said, 'not that sort of snake, but thank you anyway,' and continued my search.

When I reached reception, I was so intent on finding my quarry that I didn't immediately notice a number of clients waiting. Realising that my behaviour might seem strange, I announced, 'Excuse me, I'm sorry to bother you, but I'm looking for a snake.' Immediately grasping the absurdity of that, I laughed, and fortunately so did they.

I went to our clever, pretty receptionist, loved by all our clients. Tracy favoured the outrageous end of the latest fashion spectrum, which suited her slim figure and always made a talking point. If she had a fault it was a turn for sarcasm, which I'm sorry to say I think she picked up from me. 'Tracy,' I said, 'was this bag empty when it was brought in?'

'I don't know,' said Tracy, 'I didn't look inside. When I took it upstairs it was quite heavy.'

'Do me a favour. Pick the bag up now and tell me if it weighs the same,' I asked.

She gave me a quizzical look, but decided to humour me and did it. 'Oh no,' she said, 'it was much heavier than this.'

'Thanks very much,' I said. 'You haven't seen anything that looks rather greasy, about five feet in length, have you?'

'Yes,' she said, sarcasm surfacing. 'In Wilf's room. One of Sean Page's mates come to see him about some conveyancing.'

'I didn't mean a human being,' I said. 'I meant a constricting non-venomous reptile which crushes its prey by compression.'

'What?' asked Tracy.

'Never mind,' I said.

I dialled a number on the telephone. Someone picked up: 'Yeah?'

'Is that Albert?' I asked. 'It's Steve Smith here. I take it you're still looking for Elliott?'

'Yeah.'

'The golf bag wouldn't happen to be red with a brass zip and a gold-coloured side strap, would it?'

'Yeah, you haven't found it?' asked Albert, his voice raised in hope.

'Yeah,' I replied.

'Reet,' said Albert. 'I'm on me way, our Morris'll run me in.'

I put the telephone down. Elliott had clearly gone for a slither somewhere around my office, and it was my duty to find him before he frightened some unsuspecting person to death – particularly as our insurance wouldn't cover such an eventuality.

Just then I heard a loud cry from Wilf's office. I recognised the voice, and went in to find Pagey jumping up and down as though on fire, trying to wrench a boa constrictor from his left arm and shouting: 'Get this thing off me!'

No doubt it's reprehensible, but I dissolved into laughter, and it wasn't long before Wilf and Pagey's five-foot greasy friend joined in. Pagey wasn't laughing, though. He was fighting to keep Elliott from moving up his arm towards his neck.

'He's only being friendly,' I said, doubled up. All Pagey could say was, 'Get him off, get him off,' with one or two expletives thrown in. Pagey wasn't normally given to bad language, but Elliott had obviously upset him.

'Get him off,' he cried, sweat pouring from his brow as Wilf and I and Pagey's friend guffawed. 'You bastards, get this thing off!'

'I'm not touching it, I hate snakes,' Wilf chortled. Wilf had curly hair, which got unruly when he went too long between haircuts, and a Vandyke beard which he claimed he grew to cover his double chin. He was into coloured shirts and corresponding ties, and loved a drink, but playing football in our regular Wednesday games kept his weight down – that is, until his sports career ended when everything went south.

Pagey's friend was too convulsed with laughter to do anything, and unfortunately for the hapless Page, I didn't feel disposed to get involved either. Then I remembered that Roy Bennett had served in Burma and would therefore know all about snakes and how to deal with them. I called him, but he said he'd been more frightened of the snakes than of the Japanese. 'I couldn't go near the bloody things – they haunted my life out in Burma, they were everywhere, in the rooms, under the bed, even in the latrines. You couldn't sit down to mind your own business without worrying.'

As Elliott moved further towards Pagey's shoulder, the snake seemed to tighten his grip, and his tongue flickered from side to side expectantly. Pagey's furious shouts changed to quiet pleas. 'Get the sodding thing off,' he begged.

I could think of nothing to say or do, save, 'Here, Elliott, here, boy, here, Elliott, come on, lad, good boy.'

Pagey looked at me in disgust. 'You bloody idiot. GET... IT... OFF... ME.'

By this time Elliott's face was almost in line with Pagey's neck. 'Oh Christ,' he said, 'it's going to kill me.'

Wilf and I considered the situation. On the one hand, if we interfered the snake might turn on us; on the other, if Elliott did choke Pagey we would naturally feel responsible.

'Give him a hand,' I said to Wilf. 'Help him, for God's sake.'

Wilf looked at me in astonishment. 'You help him. I hate snakes.'

'Bugger that for a game of soldiers,' I said. 'The owner's on his way, he should be here in a few minutes.'

'Bloody marvellous,' said Pagey. 'The bastard'll have killed me by then. Just cut its head off or something.'

'With what?' I asked.

'What about a knife?' said Pagey. 'Or hit it.'

His hand had begun to turn blue; Elliott was turning on the pressure. We watched as though hypnotised.

'Don't worry, Pagey, it's not poisonous,' I said weakly.

He looked at me in disgust. 'No, you moron, it'll have crushed me to death before it gets to poison me. That's a great relief, I can assure you.'

At that moment, fortunately, Albert walked in, concern for Elliott etched all over his face, and immediately took charge. He went over to Pagey and said, 'Don't panic. Tha's upsetting 'im.'

'*I'm* upsetting *him*?' spluttered Pagey. 'What do you think he's doing to me? Ouch!'

Albert weaved his magic spell by stroking the snake's head and whispering lovingly to it – which impressed Pagey even less. But within moments, he had Elliott in his arms and around his waist. ''E's only being friendly,' he told Pagey, reproachfully. ''E's soft as they cum.'

'He's a nightmare,' said Pagey, beginning to recover. 'The bloody thing ought to be put down. Just look at its crap on my arm,' he moaned, as he noticed streams of gooey liquid along his sleeve.

'That proves 'e likes thee,' said Albert. 'They won't shit unless they're comfy.'

Pagey pointed to his own bottom and said, 'Yes, and I like him like I adore piles. You ought to have a licence for that thing.' Unlike the rest of us, he would not see the funny side – but then, we hadn't been the object of a snake's affection.

Albert asked who had returned the bag, but we were unable to tell him.

'I don't suppose they've left the fags?' he said.

'No,' I said. Nevertheless, Albert was delighted to be reunited with his friend Elliott. The Heptonstall grin was back, wider than ever, as he walked across the churchyard to catch the bus home.

We closed the office and adjourned to the Cross Keys, our local, for a bar meal and some liquid refreshment, where we were soon joined by Jarvis and our handyman friend Bodger Broom. I ordered the first round: gins for Wilf and me, a large brandy for Jarvis, a pint of lager for Bodger – and a 'snakebite' for Pagey.

Three days later, my client Tank reappeared before the magistrates, having been cleared of burglary for lack of forensic evidence. However, he had admitted the offences involving motor vehicles (including the theft of a Transit van), and since he'd been on bail at the time was facing custody for sure.

When I visited him in the cells he was resigned to his fate. I was impressed with his philosophical attitude. It's always easier when defendants take advice, because you can do a much better job for them. With Tank accepting the inevitable, I was able to prepare what we could by way of mitigation, be realistic with the bench and keep the sentence down to a minimum.

Tank was duly given a three-month sentence, and as I took my leave of him in the cells below the court, I said, 'By the way, Tank, there was one thing I wanted to ask you before I go.'

'Ask away,' said Tank. 'It looks like I'll be here for a while.'

'Those marks on your neck – how did you get them?'

Tank laughed, and shrugged. 'Steve,' he said, 'I'll tell you, but you'll never believe it!'

And do you know – he was wrong…

TWO

GARY'S BROTHER'S DEAF

The case of Gary Wilkes troubled me more than most. During my career I have often been disappointed with the court's decisions, which isn't unusual if you care about what you are doing. But in this case the truth was hidden by the one person I would have expected to want it to come out.

Gary Wilkes was in his mid-twenties. At just over six foot, with a broad, athletic build, he could look after himself. He had strong, pointed features, dark eyes, a mass of curly jet-black hair, almost like a gypsy, and large ears with long lobes, one of them lower than the other.

His younger brother Richie was about the same height but with a more wiry build. There was a strong family resemblance, but Richie had sadly been born deaf, which often led to misunderstandings and frustration, manifested in outbursts of temper. Gary, who was devoted to his brother, always looked after him among outsiders, who only knew that he had a very short fuse.

On April Fool's Day 1983, the brothers went to their local for a drink and a game of pool. That day there was a man at the bar whose appearance made him stand out from the regulars, a thickset lad with a skinhead haircut, wearing a denim shirt, jeans and Doc Martens: Gary remembered thinking he looked 'dead handy'. About 3 pm, when Gary and Richie were finishing their game, the skinhead apparently became impatient to play, and slammed his twenty pence down on the side of the pool table just as Richie was preparing his shot. The brothers then had some difficulty playing the final ball, which set the skinhead to drumming his fingers on the side of the table and sighing exaggeratedly, but eventually the black was potted, much to Richie's joy.

'About time,' said the skinhead forcefully. 'You want to learn to play properly.'

Richie, who had his back to him, made no reply, for obvious reasons, which inflamed the stranger further. 'Are you fucking deaf as well as fucking hopeless?' he shouted.

At this stage Gary intervened. 'He is deaf, as a matter of fact, and he's not done anything to you. If you want the table, here it is.'

'Right, bastard,' said the skinhead, 'I'm fucking sick of you. Outside: we'll sort this out out there.'

'Look,' said Gary, 'we don't want any trouble. You've got the table; start playing and leave us alone.'

With that, the skinhead grabbed Gary and pushed him out of the door. Richie ran after them, as did the landlord, Archie. But by the time Archie got there, the skinhead was on the ground, bleeding from his mouth and ear. An ambulance was called, and with it came the Rotherham police. Within half an hour, Gary and Richie were at the police station.

The police couldn't interview Richie without an interpreter, so he was allowed to go home once a date for that had been fixed. The skinhead was still unconscious, so Gary was the only participant interviewed. This was before the 1984 Police and Criminal Evidence Act prompted interviews to take place in the presence of a solicitor, and he was questioned alone. He admitted hitting the skinhead and rendering him unconscious, saying that he had struck out in self-defence and that Richie had had nothing to do with the incident. When the skinhead recovered, he had no recollection of what had happened after he went into the pub – a type of amnesia fairly common after head injuries, but especially convenient in this case.

Gary came to see me just before his first court appearance. 'I want to plead not guilty because I was defending myself. I had no alternative but to hit him,' he said, with the air of a man who had been well rehearsed.

I didn't have the prosecution evidence at that stage, but based on what he told me, I thought Gary had a reasonable case; it seemed that we were dealing with a yob who'd simply got more than he bargained for. Gary gave me the names of three witnesses who would testify to the yob's behaviour in the pub, but unfortunately I had no one who could give evidence about the incident outside.

The prosecution served their evidence on me: statements from the complainant and a heavily pregnant lady who had been standing at a nearby bus stop when the incident took place, together with the transcripts of the police interviews with Gary and the skinhead. Despite his amnesia, the latter now claimed he'd been attacked without provocation: he said he'd only joined the queue by putting his money on the pool table, that Richie had pushed it off, and when he had remonstrated, he had been dragged outside and beaten up. All this we could counter – but the incident outside was the basis of the charge.

The lady at the bus stop had stated that she saw three men arguing outside the pub, and then one man hit the skinhead repeatedly about the face and head. She couldn't give a clear description of the attacker, but seemed certain that it was the skinhead who was attacked, not the other way around: we would need to dent the credibility of this evidence to have a good chance of an acquittal.

In his police interview, Gary had said, among other things, 'He attacked me, so I hit him.' He then went on to say that he aimed a further two blows at the face, which worried me, because the rule of self-defence specifies that you are only entitled to use a proportional amount of force to that used against you. Clearly, if there came a time when the skinhead's attack ceased and Gary hit him again, he couldn't claim to be still defending himself. But if he said he anticipated a further attack, his action would be permissible – the law doesn't require you to be attacked before you take action. We certainly had a case to argue, and I believed that if the yob could be shown for what he was, we had a reasonable chance in front of a fair bench, assuming the lady's evidence could be put in doubt.

I interviewed our three witnesses, all perfectly reputable and with no reason to lie. The first was the barmaid, who was rather sympathetic to our cause, as it seemed that the yob had been rude to her before the incident with Gary. The second, a friend of the brothers of good character who had been waiting his turn to play pool, was quite definite that the yob had been out looking for trouble. The third witness was probably our key one, a sixtyish regular at the pub who had been seated at the bar throughout the whole incident, and gave almost identical evidence to the other two.

I wanted to interview Richie, but Gary showed a marked reluctance to involve him.

'But Gary, his evidence may be helpful,' I stressed.

'But he can't hear, and he'd be really embarrassed if he's got to perform sign language in front of a room full of strangers,' replied Gary. 'I don't want him involved. He'd only get upset, and when he does, he... No, I don't want to put him through it, my mind's made up. We've got the three other witnesses and that should be enough, shouldn't it?' he asked, looking for my agreement.

'They only saw the incident inside. Your charge is on the one outside, on which we don't have any witnesses at all. That's why I want to call Richie.'

'No, sorry,' said Gary, and sat back with his arms folded in a gesture of finality.

'Look, Gary, it's your case and you can run it how you want, but I have to advise you that I'm not prepared to accept responsibility for running it without the main witness. If you get convicted, it'll be your fault, not mine.'

'I'll accept that,' said Gary, and I reluctantly yielded.

The trial had been scheduled for a full day, and when I arrived at court I found that it would be heard by a visiting stipendiary magistrate. There are two kinds of magistrates: lay magistrates, who aren't legally qualified, and usually sit as a panel of three, advised on the law by the clerk to the court; and stipendiary magistrates, who are qualified solicitors or barristers, and usually sit alone and make the legal decisions themselves. It is often suggested that your chances of success in a trial are much less in front of a stipendiary, and certainly they're often less helpful to the defence, because they've usually heard more of the excuses before. But on this occasion the choice of a stipendiary really dampened my enthusiasm, since while the court preliminaries were being dealt with, Gary leaned across to me and whispered that he'd been sentenced by the same magistrate for another offence some two years ago.

I doubted if the stipendiary would remember – they deal with so many cases in a week, let alone two years – but I was honour-bound to mention the matter to him so he could decide whether to retire gracefully or not. In the event, he was a deputy looking for a full-time appointment who didn't want to blot his copybook in any way so, erring on the side of caution, he disqualified himself from sitting, and a fresh bench of lay magistrates was drafted in from another court.

The chairman glowered at me as he entered the courtroom. This perplexed me, because I had always thought I got on very well with him, until the clerk told me he had only expected to sit until 1 pm, and had a council meeting he didn't want to miss at 2.30pm. Understandably if unfortunately, the thought of dealing with an all-day trial got up his nose.

I tried to redeem the situation by expressing my regret that the bench had been inconvenienced, and the Crown Prosecution

Service man, my old friend Neil Franklin, sent me a little note with the words 'F*****g creep' written on it, before standing and agreeing with me. The chairman grunted in disapproval as my client was called back into court and repeated his plea of not guilty, and I began to wish I'd stuck with the stipendiary.

The complainant came in to give evidence, his head bald apart from about a centimetre's growth of hair. I was relying on the fact that he was a skinhead to push home the suggestion that all such people were yobs. Of course, that isn't true any longer, because all manner of people now adopt that particular hairstyle, but in the early 'eighties the look signalled 'yob'. He read the oath as though the handling of a Bible was the most onerous task ever, and the case began.

He recounted his story faithfully according to his statement, all the time eying me across the oak-panelled courtroom with suspicion. Neil Franklin, an extremely experienced prosecutor who now enjoys high office in West Yorkshire, did his job to the letter, although I suspect without much pleasure. Then it was my turn to cross-examine.

I rose to my feet, and we stared at each other like boxers before the opening bell. It was clear he viewed me as representing something for which he had no respect whatsoever. The feeling was mutual.

'You are a skinhead, are you not?' I asked fearlessly.

'Depends what you mean by skinhead,' came the capable answer. Round one to the yob.

'A skinhead is a youth with his hair cut almost down to the wood, who believes that violence and disorder are acceptable codes of behaviour, yes?' I asked forcefully.

'Not at all,' came the reply. 'You can't generalise. Most solicitors are money-grabbers oblivious to the dictates of society or its members, particularly those who aren't lucky enough to be in the same class.' Round two to Karl Marx. This was going to be a battle of wills, so I tried to move on to a more direct approach.

'You were looking for trouble?'

'No,' came the reply.

'You were indiscriminate so far as your bad conduct was concerned?'

'No,' he repeated. The yob had been schooled in how to answer questions, and was leaving virtually no opening for me to cross-examine.

'The defendant will say that you were ill-mannered and aggressive.'

'Denied,' said the yob.

'Is the defendant lying or mistaken?'

'Lying,' came the reply, leaving me the opening I was looking for.

'There are three independent witnesses who all say your behaviour was loutish and aggressive. Are they lying too?'

'Yes. They look after their own in that pub.'

'You told a woman in the bar to shift from the pool table. Shift. No please, no thank you, just shift. That's not very polite, is it?'

'So what?' I was beginning to get behind his guard.

'You swore at the two lads playing pool because you thought they were taking their time?'

'Yes. They were.'

'You didn't mention swearing in your statement to the police.'

'I must have forgot, but that doesn't give him the right to attack me.'

'Quite, but there's no excuse for grabbing someone by the throat either, is there? The witnesses say you did that.'

'I was defending myself. They attacked me.'

'The barmaid will say that she served you with pints of lager on at least eight occasions. The other witnesses I referred to earlier all speak of you being drunk – what do you say about that?'

'They're lying. I'm used to lager, it doesn't make me drunk.'

'Not only were you drunk, but you were aggressive and spoiling for a fight, or so the witnesses say. They're not lying – you are.' There was no answer, so I continued, 'Do you remember slamming money on the pool table?'

'No.'

'Then I'm sorry to tell you the witnesses have lied again – they say you did.'

'I put the money down – that's how you register for a game. It may have sounded like slamming.'

'When a player is taking a shot? And you have agreed you grabbed my client's throat.'

'In self-defence. And who knocked me out, the man in the moon?'

Progress! 'Can you remember anything of the incident outside?' I continued.

'Just being hit, that's all.'

'So it could have been either of the young men who hit you?' I had an opening, and pursued it for all I was worth. 'Could you argue if I said, for example, it was the younger and smaller of the two men, the one with the hearing aid?'

'No, but I know I was hit.'

'All right, but you can't say who hit you or how it happened, can you?'

'Would you, being unconscious for three days?'

'No, I dare say I wouldn't have a clue.'

'Exactly,' said the youth.

'Exactly,' I agreed, and sat down, my point made. If he couldn't say who hit him or in what circumstances, how could the prosecution prove assault?

The next witness was the crucial lady at the bus stop, who was about eight and a half months pregnant and looked a little hot under the collar. The chairman politely asked her to sit down to give her evidence, promising that it wouldn't take long – with a stare at me that said menacingly, 'It won't, will it?'

She described seeing three men come out of the pub, and then a fight.

'How many of them fought?' asked Neil.

'I'm not sure. I think all of them – two definitely, and another got involved.'

'How did it end?'

'The youth with the crew-cut ended up on the floor. He banged his head when he fell, a nasty bump. I didn't expect him to get up, and he didn't.'

Neil sat down, and I got up to cross-examine. The lady had no axe to grind, and was just doing her best to be truthful, so I smiled at her and asked if she wouldn't mind answering a few questions to put her at ease.

'You saw a fight, and very fairly said that you're not sure how many fought. Is that because you didn't see them all exchange blows?'

'Well, yes, I suppose so.'

'Could it be that two men were fighting and one was trying to break them up?'

'It could have been. It wasn't clear, it happened so quickly. One minute he was on his feet, then he was down.'

'Enough for one blow and that was it?'

'Maybe. I wouldn't like to say,' she said thoughtfully. 'There was a lot of shouting, and the next minute the young man was on the floor.'

'Who was shouting?' I asked.

'When they first came out, him with the crew-cut was.'

'How did they all come outside?' I took a risk here, because the yob had claimed he was dragged out, but jogging her memory might go in my favour.

'Walked. He was shouting, the short-haired one, then there was a fight.'

'Did you see the first blow? Could you be sure the short-haired youth wasn't the aggressor?'

'Not really. He was certainly doing the shouting. He was angry.'

'Angry enough to hit out?'

'I should say so,' she replied.

I then committed the cardinal sin of any advocate – asking one question too many. 'Which of the other lads fought?'

I'd worked out my move: if she said Gary, I'd claim self-defence, and if she said Richie, I'd say Gary shouldn't have been charged; if she wasn't sure, the prosecution hadn't proven their case.

'I think it was the smaller of the two.'

Then the truth hit me. I knew why Gary didn't want his brother to give evidence. I thanked the witness and sat down, trying not to look as if I was in a hurry.

Neil rose to re-examine and plug the holes I'd made in his case, but luckily, at that moment the witness cried out: 'Oh! My waters have broken!'

There was instant consternation: a police officer was called and our witness hastily dispatched to the maternity wing of the local hospital. (At 7:30 pm she became the proud mother of a bouncing baby girl she named Verity, because she said that the truth very nearly came out in Rotherham court that day.) From my point of view, the timing was perfect; the gaps would remain unplugged.

Once the courtroom calmed down; I decided to argue that the case should not proceed for the following reasons: first, the skin-head's evidence didn't explain how the incident had occurred; second, he conceded that he didn't know who had hit him; and third, the bus-stop lady had described him as the aggressor and Richie as the one responsible for the blow. The chairman was keen to leave, and here was his ideal opportunity.

The magistrates retired, and fifteen minutes later sent for the clerk. This was not a good sign, because I expected that he would persuade them to refuse the submission. I was right, so the trial had to continue.

I called my client into the witness box. Gary stood up to cross-examination very well, and my three witnesses made it abundantly clear that the skinhead had been aggressively drunk. The barmaid was magnificent: knowing neither Gary nor Richie, she was obviously independent, described the skinhead's rudeness to her, said that he had frightened her and Gary had interceded, asking him to leave her alone. She ended her evidence by saying the skinhead had grabbed Gary by the throat and pushed him outside. When Neil cross-examined her, she gave a good account of herself, and I felt that we were in the home straight. A good summing-up speech from me and we'd cracked it.

I waxed lyrical about the yob culture, and reminded the bench that Gary had tried to keep the peace: if he was guilty of anything, it was remonstrating with the skinhead for his threatening behaviour to a lady. The bench nodded approvingly, and I concluded: 'If the complainant can't remember what happened, and if the other prosecution witness agrees that he was the aggressor, how can you convict the defendant of assault? And even if you feel he has been assaulted, by whom?' I left it at that, and they retired. We'd walked it, as far as I was concerned.

'What do you think, Steve?' asked Gary.

'If I were a gambler, Gary, I'd say it's a one-horse race, but I've done the job long enough not to make predictions.'

Our conversation was interrupted by a buzzer on the clerk's desk. The clerk disappeared, and returned to announce that the bench had a question he thought best asked in open court: 'How did the complainant get to the public house?'

Neil looked as amazed as I felt. 'What's that got to do with it?' he asked. The clerk said there was no evidence on that point, and the chairman had asked if any could be called. Neil said that we had both finished our cases, so the evidence was closed, and the bench retired again.

'Don't worry,' said Neil. 'You're home and dry. That isn't relevant.'

It was more than half an hour before the bench came back in. They looked away from Gary, which was a bad omen, and the chairman announced: 'We find the case proved, you're guilty of assault...'

I didn't catch the end of it, staring at them in complete bewilderment.

The skinhead punched the air and shouted 'Yes!' from the back of the court. The chairman then asked me, 'Do you wish to say anything, Mr Smith?'

I had to summon every ounce of self-discipline not to embarrass myself with unsuitable expletives, but just shook my head and bit my lip so angrily I drew blood; Neil simply raised his eyebrows and looked away. I glanced to the back of the courtroom, and saw from Richie's expression that he'd realised his brother had been found guilty, although Gary was innocent. But Richie...

The chairman announced, 'In view of your criminal record, we feel that a prison sentence is appropriate. You will therefore go to prison for six months.'

I threw my pen down in disgust, but Gary raised a smile for me, and waved to Richie before disappearing down the spiral staircase to the cells. And there was nothing to be done about it: the bench had acted contrary to all the norms of lay magistrates, but their word was, literally, law.

The court emptied, leaving me and Richie alone. He was confused, but I knew he could sense my anger. He asked just a one-word question: 'Prison?'

'Yes,' I nodded, and held up six fingers. 'But he'll serve...' and this time I kept three fingers raised.

'Wrong,' said Richie.

'Yes, I know,' I replied. I also knew that I'd made one of the biggest mistakes you can in this job: taking the results personally. But looking at Richie, sitting there friendless and confused, I couldn't help it. I hate dealing with cases when the courts get it wrong. Fortunately, it doesn't happen very often.

My thoughts were interrupted by Richie's strained voice. 'It's wrong,' he said. 'Not him.'

'Yes, I know,' I replied, mouthing each word carefully. 'It was you, wasn't it?'

'Yes, me,' he replied.

'Well, we can appeal, but if we do the court will have to know the truth. That will mean they know Gary's committed perjury, which is eighteen months at least for him, and conspiracy to pervert for you as well. Somehow I don't think we'll be appealing, do you?'

Richie hung his head.

I saw Gary afterwards. He had no complaints about my handling of the case, but I had plenty about being misled. I also couldn't understand the magistrates' decision, unless they had picked up on the fact he was lying when he gave evidence – in which case they'd got it right, but for the wrong reasons.

And it was 5.30 pm, and I had a football match at six. We lost. Another injustice, I thought. It just hadn't been my day.

THREE

SUKI DEVILLE AND THE CASE OF THE SILVER CHALICE SAUNA

Suki Deville was what's called a high-class call girl. I've never understood what one might consider high-class about that profession, but she was certainly very attractive, with only a hint of the prostitute about her. She came into my office one late spring afternoon as I was about to leave to play our regular Wednesday game of football – Bader Lidster and 'Club 'em' Darker (who as you might guess from the nickname was handy with his fists) were waiting in reception for me.

'I won't keep you long, lads,' I said, inviting Miss Deville into my room. She was tall, with jet-black hair and unusually deep blue eyes, a Colgate smile which indicated that she must have eaten calcium with every meal and spent the rest of the day brushing her teeth. The thing I noticed most, however, was a small diamond set into one of her front teeth, slightly off-centre.

'I'm in trouble with the DSS,' she said in a pleasant voice with a hotel receptionist's twang and a slight Scottish accent. 'They say I signed on and received unemployment benefit while working.'

She opened her Gucci handbag and passed me the summonses, folded immaculately in a scented envelope simply addressed to 'The Solicitor'. I looked at the charges, which seemed to relate to a period of over eighteen months. The Department of Social Security was saying that Miss Deville had claimed approximately £3,000 she wasn't entitled to. Because of the amount of money involved, my pretty client was staring into the unwelcome arms of Her Majesty's Prison New Hall.

'What do you think I'll get?' asked Miss Deville, so matter-of-factly I was disconcerted. Most clients find it difficult even to talk about their charges at first, let alone the probable penalties, but she was clearly a tough cookie.

'Are you pleading guilty?' I asked.

'I don't think I have any option; I've admitted it,' she said coolly.

'Well in that case, we'll ask the court to be as lenient as possible. But we're dealing with quite a lot of money, so they're bound to take a serious view.'

Often defendants have no real conception of how serious their case is, and since their defence solicitor is first in the firing line when the waste material hits the fan, it's better to leave them in no doubt about what might happen at the end of the day. It isn't easy to gauge just when to impart the bad news, but this particular defendant was intelligent and tough, so I thought it prudent to let her know from the outset that imprisonment was a real possibility.

After a sharp intake of breath, she asked me how long. I said, 'Three months, of which you'll serve six weeks.'

'Is there no prospect of a suspended sentence?' she asked.

'There's always the prospect, but immediate prison is more likely than not.'

'When will it happen?' she asked.

'You're due to appear in court at the end of the month, on the date contained in the summons. Since you intend to plead guilty, they'll probably adjourn your case for a probation report before sentencing. In the circumstances, I think you have eight weeks to organise your affairs.'

After giving that bad news, I took the details of the case and the mitigation we were to put forward. It seemed that Miss Deville had told the DSS she was unemployed, and was accordingly granted social security benefit, but it had come to the attention of the DSS investigators that for a substantial period she had been working as a hostess in a sauna/health club in the Nottingham area on a self-employed basis, paying 'rent' of £100 a week to the owners for the use of their facilities. She told me that a number of other girls had similar arrangements there.

I was curious to know how she had been found out, but she was unable to help. I said I would try to discover the answer, if only to satisfy my own curiosity, and made an appointment for the following week to complete my instruction.

As I showed Miss Deville to the door, Lidster was inspecting his foot for signs of his septic toe problem recurring. Miss Deville looked, shuddered and headed for the outer door; I turned back to the others and we set off to the match. We were beaten comprehensively by a local pub team who, according to Bader, were fielding three ringers, one of whom, the goalkeeper, had played league football professionally. We tried everything to get past him, but failed miserably, finally losing 4–0.

The next day, on my way to the magistrates' court, I met the solicitor who prosecuted for the DSS. I mentioned that I was interested to know how they'd got involved in my new client's case, particularly since Miss Deville had been working well outside the area where she was claiming benefits. According to him, she had been found out quite by chance, as is often the case: she had been 'clocked', as the criminals call it, in the Nottingham sauna and then recognised while signing on in Rotherham – the diamond in the tooth was the giveaway. I suppose there aren't many people with jewelled teeth, and as she was particularly pretty girl, she would stand out in a crowd.

My prosecutor friend couldn't tell me who had shopped her: just that the information came, as it normally does, from 'an informant'. But that informant certainly had a lot of information about, and insight into, the workings of the Silver Chalice Sauna.

I also found it strange that the informant had, as well as Suki, connections with both Rotherham DSS and Nottingham.

I was at court to represent a number of ne'er-do-wells, including Barry Baldwin from Bolton-on-Dearne, an ex-serviceman and secretary of a local working men's club, who had been caught by the police driving over the prescribed limit. Barry had lost his papers, and couldn't remember exactly what the drink-drive reading was, so I took some details from him, intending to ask for an adjournment until I had a better picture of the trouble that he was in.

All went well until the clerk of the court, who could be best described as a 'pompous shit', produced some papers which showed that Barry had been before the court in the past for drunk-driving, and hadn't paid off all the fines. He asked me if I was aware of this, and I told him that my crystal ball was broken. The clerk promptly called Barry into the witness box to give evidence as to his means. Understandably Barry was nervous, because the clerk had mentioned the possibility of him going to prison for being in default.

With the gusto of a prosecutor *manqué*, the clerk laid into Barry. 'I am going to make a note of what you say. I am going to ask you various questions, and I would like you to direct your answers to the magistrates sitting behind me. I will then give you the opportunity to make any comments you wish, either yourself or through your solicitor, and the court will then decide whether or not you are so far in default that only a prison sentence is appropriate. If you are, I can tell you that the period you will be sentenced to will be not less than fourteen days. Do you understand?'

Barry took a deep breath and said, 'Pardon?'

The clerk repeated the same rigmarole, word for word. 'Pardon?' said a confused Barry again.

The court clerk, losing patience, shouted at the top of his voice, 'Are you deaf?' To which Barry replied, 'Yes.'

'Well then, I'll shout. Do you have a hearing aid?'

Barry replied with aplomb, 'I'm sorry, I forgot to bring it.'

The court clerk duly shouted his message, and concluded by saying, 'In so far as you can, keep one eye on the magistrates and one eye on my pen.'

'I've only got one eye,' said Barry. 'Where does tha want me to point it?'

Laughter rang round the room, and the clerk realised he had lost. Barry was ordered to pay his fines at the rate of £5 a week, and allowed to leave the court. All the solicitors waiting their turn were delighted that he had got one over this most unpopular of the court clerks.

I took Barry into the rat-hole interview room to discuss our plan of attack, and for the first time noticed a very thin wire leading from a small object in his right ear. 'You really are deaf!' I said.

'Only when this isn't switched on,' he grinned.

We agreed to meet at court for the adjourned hearing, and as Barry turned to leave, I realised it might be in his interests to produce a copy of his war record. Barry, who was in his late sixties, had served in the Second World War – which was how he had lost his eye – and still had his military bearing, though he had lost the battle with his ever-increasing waistline. I called his name, and he turned back unhesitatingly.

'Still switched on, then, Barry?' I asked with a smile, and he smiled back but didn't answer. I asked him to bring his army record to court next time, and off he marched. I remember I thought how straightforward he was to deal with.

Walking back to the office, I met the investigator on the DSS case against Suki Deville, and took the opportunity to ask him about her; he was a pleasant chap, and as she was pleading guilty I saw no harm in speaking to him. He told me that they had received information from an unimpeachable source who had first-hand knowledge of where she was working, but declined to comment further. There was no statement in the evidence explaining the position, and as she had made a confession I couldn't expect one, so it looked as though my curiosity would go unsatisfied.

The following week, Miss Deville came in to see me again. I caught sight of her alighting from a sports Mercedes outside my office; I couldn't see the driver, but the car looked as though it had only just left the showroom.

This time Miss Deville seemed extremely anxious, and before I could say anything she asked: 'You won't discuss this case with anyone, will you?'

'Of course not in any way that might compromise you, but I may have to discuss it with people connected with the court proceedings—'

'I didn't mean that,' she interrupted. 'I meant if someone phones and asks about me or tries to find out why I came here.'

Perhaps the man in the Mercedes didn't know the real reason for her calling on me, I thought. I reassured her, and began to sort out the question of costs. She told me she didn't believe she was eligible for legal aid, and was ready to pay her costs privately. Trusting soul that I am, I asked for them up front.

'Let's get that sorted straight away,' she said, pulling a large wad of £20 notes, fresh from the bank with their paper band still on, from her handbag. She paid the agreed amount, and I wrote out a receipt.

'I'm not working at the sauna now,' she said. 'I packed that in. I've some savings, and when they run out I'll decide what to do.'

She seemed keen to delay the case. As I hadn't received any evidence at that stage, and would need time to consider it when I did, I argued for, and got, an adjournment of four weeks. We had one more meeting before the court date was fixed, and again Suki's anxiety about the final date of her case, and the question of secrecy, haunted her conversation. I wondered if her lack of previous convictions had something to do with her obvious fear of appearing at court, but the fear of publicity seemed to be uppermost in her mind.

On her second appearance, Suki was the centre of attention as she waited outside Court Number 3. She was not only attractive, but extremely smartly dressed, sticking out like a sore thumb among the rapscallions in a similar plight – such as Lavinia Broughton, another DSS fraudster I was representing that morning. Lavinia was a teenager from a regular client family of mine whom I hadn't met before, but I knew her parents and elder siblings very well.

Lavinia was by no means nervous as she took large puffs from her Park Drive cigarette underneath the sign saying 'NO SMOKING IN THIS AREA'. I introduced myself and took her to the end of corridor, just outside the Magistrates' Retiring Room, for there was no rat-hole outside Court Number 3. The security was non-existent, and magistrates were almost certain to come into contact with defendants – how times have changed with the new purpose-built courts and tradesmen's entrance for the judiciary!

'How many charges have you got, Miss Broughton?' I asked.

'Four, and twenty-five TICs,' replied this self-assured defendant.

I completed the legal aid forms, which in itself was quite a feat, as there was no desk, and not even a window ledge to rest it on, and passed them to her for signature, along with an old biro. (I had learned the hard way not to offer any of my cherished fountain pens, as many defendants had never used one and invariably twisted the nib or complained that it wouldn't write.) As she wrote out her name in full, I tried to hurry her along by saying, 'Just use your initial for your Christian names.' I thought 'Lavinia Avril Jeanette Mary Louise Enid Broughton' was a veritable novel, but she wrote it in full anyway, on three separate places on two forms.

As she was writing, I said, 'It's an unusual name, Lavinia. What do your friends call you? Is it Tina or Tine or Tin or Tie?'

'No, none of those. They call me Lav,' she replied, without a hint of embarrassment. I didn't ask her to explain why.

The contrast between her and Suki couldn't have been wider. On the one hand I had Suki, the dazzling beauty with designer clothes and a brothel for a retreat, and on the other poor old Lav, plain and untidy, wearing cheap clothes and designer-second trainers from the local market, but whose morals had been fashioned by prudish parents and an absence of desire from the local males.

Both ladies became subject to consideration by the probation service, and their cases were adjourned for four weeks for their reports. Miss Deville was first in to see the probation officer, while Lav waited outside. As Suki emerged she came face to face with Lav for a split second, and I couldn't help noticing the look of disgust on both faces – I suspect for entirely different reasons.

Three weeks later the probation service rang to tell me that Miss Deville had failed to attend two appointments; their second letter had been returned marked 'GONE AWAY'. The next day, my letter to her confirming the hearing date was also returned with the same message, and the court duly issued a warrant for her arrest. Approximately a month after that, I received an airmail letter from a Mrs Suki Dorchester-Hall, sent from the Hilton Hotel, New York. It read:

Dear Mr Smith,

Thank you for your valuable assistance in completing my legal affairs in England. I am pleased to report that, on 1 September, Guy Dorchester-Hall and I were married here in New York. Guy is now resident here with a full American passport. Fortunately or unfortunately, depending upon which way you look at it, I will be unable to return owing to my commitments here.

In the circumstances, please close my file but keep it by you in the unlikely event of my return. I would be grateful if you would not disclose my whereabouts to any interested parties.

If my husband and I can place any work with you in England, we will be pleased so to do.

With kindest regards.
SUKI DORCHESTER-HALL

Six months on, I was making a rare appearance in the Nottingham Magistrates' Court on behalf of a haulage contractor who had got himself into difficulties with an insecure load on the motorway in the Nottingham area. Mick was a good driver, but as some haulage contractors do, he lived his working life rather close to the wind, and sometimes found himself falling foul of the dreaded Construction and Use Regulations.

Normally I would instruct agents to appear on my behalf in a 'foreign' town, but this was the fourth time in a year Mick had appeared in court, and he was worried that the Vehicles Tribunal in Leeds might consider taking his operator's licence away. I had a good business relationship with Mick, so when he explained he'd prefer me to attend, rather than some solicitor he'd never met before and who would squeeze his case in among his own, leaving him until the end of the list, I agreed to make the journey down the M1.

When I arrived at court, I found that the facts given by the prosecution were rather different from those supplied to me by my client, which meant a further consultation before we went into the courtroom.

'Mick, you told me it was a bumper that fell off the back of your lorry on the motorway,' I said. 'You didn't say it was still attached to the wreckage of a Ford Transit van, which blocked two carriage-ways of the M1.'

'Aarrgh, but not for long,' said Mick.

'No, because the police had it towed off. When did you first realise the vehicle had fallen from the back of your lorry?'

'When the police pulled me up. Anyroad, how do I know it was off my lorry?'

'Because two officers in the police car say they saw it fall off and had to swerve to avoid it.'

'I didn't see that in my mirror,' said Mick.

'Maybe because you hadn't got a mirror?' I replied. 'The police said it was broken.'

'Bloody hell, they're doing me for everything – it's harassment,' announced Mick, aggrieved.

It took a while to convince Mick he had no option but to plead guilty to yet another black mark against his name for the traffic commissioners to consider, and throw himself on the mercy of the court. When he reluctantly agreed, I checked the order of play with the court usher. To my dismay, he told me we were well down the list, and he doubted our case would be on before lunch: I had cases in Sheffield starting at 2.15pm, and if I wasn't there I could expect a Grade Five bollocking. I decided to do what I always do in situations like this – creep. If I put on an injured expression and told the clerk of the court the truth, he might be sympathetic and let me sneak on; even in the 'me first' eighties culture, most solicitors still prided themselves on being courteous to outsiders.

However, Nottingham was a busy court, with just too many cases in the list that day. What's more, it turned out this wasn't a Crown Prosecution Service court but a Department of Social Security one, and they had a lot of cases which they were bringing on first. 'Flipping heck,' I thought, or words to that effect.

But the clerk of the court did his best for me when I explained my plight. He persuaded the DSS to let me squeeze in after their first four cases, and advised me to stay on the solicitors' bench so as not to miss my slot, so it was by pure chance that I watched the morning's events.

The DSS cases were all people claiming benefit when they shouldn't have, and the faces all blurred into one. Then the fourth case came on. Leaving the court to alert Mick to be ready, I came face to face with the defendant, a thirtyish woman with expertly dyed and well-groomed blonde hair. It was one of those instances when both parties step aside the same way, then both correct by stepping the other way, so we were face to face for a little longer than we normally would have been and made eye contact. Her face was vaguely familiar to me, and there was no doubt that she knew me, but I couldn't place her.

I came back and sat down in time to hear the clerk go through the motions.

'Is your full name Tracey Deveraux?' he asked. I watched as she answered with a slight Scottish accent, trying to recall where I had seen her before.

The charge was that she had claimed something in the region of £2,000 in benefits whilst working for a high-class escort agency. At the end of the case there was an adjournment for the preparation of probation reports, and she was introduced to the probation officer immediately in front of me. As they shook hands she beamed a bright smile – and I noticed a diamond set in one of her front teeth, slightly off-centre. I had only ever seen anything like it once before. Her hair may have changed colour, but there was no mistaking that diamond.

The woman left the courtroom without a backward glance. I put her out of my mind and settled into Mick's case, mitigated as best as I could, and fortunately the bench was lenient; he walked out of court thinking I was a genius. I explained modestly that it was just a piece of luck, but he insisted that it was 'down to me'. Since I supposed if the luck had gone the other way that would have been down to me as well, I decided to enjoy his appreciation.

As we reached the multi-storey car park, a red Mercedes convertible drove out, to wolf-whistles from a group of labourers digging up the road nearby. 'A bit of all right, that,' said Mick.

'Yes, lovely car, I wish I had one,' I replied.

'Not the car, the bird in it,' said Mick. 'Did you clock her? She was a cracker. And you'll never guess, but she had a diamond in one of her teeth. I saw her outside the court when we were waiting to go in.'

'Really? How unusual,' I replied, and turned to look for my car.

The answer to another part of the Suki Deville case was revealed about three months later still. Having left Sheffield magistrates' court, I was driving home through a slightly seedy district when I got stuck in a traffic jam outside a so-called massage parlour. As I was waiting, its door opened and a man with a familiar face and wet hair emerged, face to face with me. He hastily turned aside, raised a handkerchief to his face as if to blow his nose, and hurried down the street, but too late: I had already recognised my friend the DSS investigator. I suppose he could have been on 'observations', although I rather doubted that his DSS expenses claim would make any reference to this particular visit. His guilty reaction told me this was quite clearly the unimpeachable source in the Suki Deville case: the only question that remains unanswered is whether or not he was acting in the course of duty. Only a visit to the premises would reveal that, so I suppose I will never know.

FOUR

GUNFIGHT AT THE WORKING MEN'S CLUB

That summer of 1984, council workers were busy watering central Rotherham's display of hanging baskets and flowering shrubs. The mornings were greeted with a gentle mist, which disappeared by lunchtime, exposing the fierce glare of the sun in a cloudless sky. At lunchtimes, jacketless men in short-sleeved shirts wandered around the town centre and the local park with their sandwiches and cans of fizzy drink, viewing the local girls resplendent in skimpy sportswear. By nightfall, the cocktail of heat and alcohol led to many a skirmish outside public houses and nightclubs.

When those ingredients are present there will always be work for people like me. Sometimes it comes from unexpected sources, and on one occasion from South Kirkby, the small mining village near Pontefract where I grew up, whose main features were a large pit and a pub for every day of the week. The local economy relied almost exclusively on the mine: if you didn't work at the pit itself, you were doing something connected with it or serving it and its people.

Bruce Johnson was thirty-eight, and had been a miner since he was seventeen. He had a good job, if you didn't count the appalling working conditions, bringing in a reasonable income, particularly if he managed to work an extra shift, and apart from 'miner's chest' he was a fairly healthy specimen. He was a little over six foot, with a shock of curly blond hair and a youthful face marred only by a boxer's nose, which found considerable favour with the local women. He kept his sixteen stone of pure muscle 'as fit as a butcher's dog' by working out with weights and running at night with his dog Goz. But Bruce's main problem was his inability to turn away from a fight.

One hot evening in mid-August, there was an entertainment at the South Kirkby Working Men's Club. Since it was also 'cheap beer night', the club had attracted a large clientele of both pleasure-seekers and drinkers, most of whom were in the concert room, which was the club's biggest. The entertainer, or 'turn' in Yorkshire parlance, was Dwight Dazzle, known during the day at the bakery where he worked as Cyril Beevers. His voice, though untrained, was a pleasant counter-tenor, and his hobby and part-time job was to sing in the local clubs the songs made famous by the Irish tenor Josef Locke. Cyril was thirty-five and prematurely bald, so he wore a toupee, which unfortunately was deficient in both fit and colour. Despite his stage outfit of black dinner jacket, ruffle-fronted shirt with red and black edgings, blue bow tie and large medallion (on close scrutiny, this bore the words 'Sheffield City Transport', but it looked good from a distance), he looked like somebody's uncle.

Success on the local club scene was measured by applause, indifference or, if the act failed, booing and abuse and, in isolated cases, even assault and battery. Dwight usually managed to achieve indifference from his audience, which was not bad for this particular club. It was expected that the 'turn' would involve four separate forays onto the stage, lasting about twenty minutes each. Introductions were usually made in the first two spots, but after that there was little point, given that the audience grew in number, restlessness and volume.

The concert secretary, otherwise known as the 'referee', was there to introduce the acts and try to keep the audience quiet during the performances. This was an almost impossible task which he tackled by switching the house lights on and off in the area of the noise, accompanied by interruptions over the house microphone while the acts were in progress. Emotive passages of songs were often interrupted by cries of 'Gi' ower, please, let t'turn get it ower with – thank you, please!' On one occasion, he even tried to help a visiting soprano with her performance by shouting into the microphone, 'Let the poor cow finish!'

This particular evening, poor old Dwight was singing his heart out against a background of 'Quiet, please!' and 'Gi' ower, let the poor bugger sing!' and the house lights flashing on and off like disco strobes. It wasn't a fitting background for the old David Whitfield song 'Cara Mia', but Dwight had seen it all before and his skin was as thick as a rhino's.

'Cara mia mine, won't you say goodbye?' he sang, as a pot-bellied customer walked in front of the stage carrying two empty pint glasses, winked at the group at a nearby table, and shouted, 'Aw reet, George?' Before the song had finished he was back with his refills, pausing again at the table he had acknowledged on the first half of the trip.

'An' are you aw reet, Stanley?' his friend greeted him.

'Well, arghh, George, apart from t'prostate. It's giving me bollocks some 'ammer, tha knows,' shouted Stanley over the pesky noise of the singer.

The audience seemed to pay more attention to Stanley's prostate than Dwight's rendition of 'Cara Mia' – but then, Stanley was standing full in the spotlight. 'It's not stopped thee supping ale!' shouted a large woman with a blue rinse, encouraged by the laughter of her friends.

As Stanley turned to reply, Dwight hit his last note with a resounding flourish. There was no applause except by the concert secretary, who stopped when his pipe fell from his mouth, hit the microphone, and caused a loud ringing noise to emanate from the loudspeaker system before it hit the floor and broke in two. 'Oh fuck,' he announced, still over the microphone, just as Dwight was taking his bow. The audience began to get up – not to give Dwight a standing ovation, but to queue for bingo tickets.

It was in this atmosphere that Bruce Johnson walked into the toilets and occupied the urinal next to fellow regular Hedley Salter. Hedley was in his late thirties, a burly, balding man with tobacco-stained false teeth, a permanent sneer, and a tendency to hit anyone he felt had looked at him the wrong way. The town bully, he was universally disliked, and feared by many. He had been drinking, and beer had loosened his tongue. Looking over into Bruce's urinal, he couldn't resist an ill-conceived comment. 'Ah dun't reckon much to that,' he said contemptuously. 'No wonder tha can't keep a bird.'

'An' wha's tha call that, then?' Bruce replied in kind, staring at his counterpart's apparatus. 'Ah've seen more head on a pint o' flat mild.'

Hedley took the comment to heart. 'Tha's nowt but a fat twat,' he said aggressively.

'Nobody calls me fat,' said Bruce, and a brawl commenced, which spilled into the concert room, where Dwight Dazzle was back on stage performing that well-known classic 'I'll take you home again, Kathleen'.

The fight was winning the ratings battle with Dwight hands down, but the singer valiantly carried on into the second verse. On the refrain of '...take you home again, Kathleen,' the concert secretary unplugged Dwight's microphone, plugged in his own and shouted, 'Eh oop, pack it in now! We're not 'evving fighting in this club – it's Kirkby, not Dodge City!' With that he replaced the performer's microphone, and Dwight continued to sing as though nothing had happened.

But the concert secretary was wrong: it was Dodge City. As Dwight sang, 'Yes, I'll take you home again...' a bottle flew onto the stage and connected with the bingo machine, Dwight having skilfully ducked out of its path. He lifted the microphone stand to let a passing bar stool find its way onto stage without damaging the sound system. Other dodges became necessary as a variety of objects joined him on the platform, including Stan, the pot-bellied man, whose refilling route had been blocked. The club began to resemble a John Wayne saloon-brawl scene.

'I'll not tell thee again!' shouted the concert secretary – correctly, since three brawling men fell against his podium, knocking the microphone from his hands.

'And I'll take you 'ome agayayayain – ow, you bastard!' shouted Dwight, reaching the end of his song as a bar stool hit the side of his head, dislodging his toupee.

In a bid to halt the fighting, the concert secretary shouted that the club was going to call a 'free house', which was an extra game of bingo without charge. Those few words managed to calm the situation within seconds, something the riot squad couldn't have managed if they had stayed there all night.

Hedley, with two black eyes, a bloody nose, and no false teeth (which had been knocked out, found and taken home by some lucky reveller), went straight to the local police station to file a complaint. Bruce, on the other hand, emerged relatively unscathed, apart from a bloody nose, which was treated by the concert secretary's wife, Betty, in the gents' toilet. One visitor raised an objection to this, only to be told, 'Gerron wi' it, it's nowt I 'aven't seen afore.'

'Arrh, but tha's not seen this wun before,' came the sparkling riposte.

'Nay, I 'aven't. I don't wear binoculars,' quipped Betty.

Back in the concert room, the concert secretary announced the 'last house', and the minute the first number was drawn there was complete silence, as though the Battle of the Gents had never occurred. Halfway through, the police arrived to find a state of complete order. They looked around, noticing people with trickles of blood running from their noses and ears, but simply wiping it away while absorbed in the numbers being called, turned round and left. Bingo is serious business in South Kirkby – much more serious than fighting.

The following morning Bruce was getting ready for work when two policemen called at his house, one young and fresh-faced, the other old and careworn. 'What's to do, Eddie?' asked Bruce, recognising the older officer.

'That feight you 'ad wi' 'Edley Salter last neet,' said Eddie. 'He's made a complaint, tha sees, so you'll 'ave to come an' put your side down. It'll not take long, and I'll give you a lift home.'

'But I'm just off to wuk,' said Bruce. 'I can't afford to miss a shift, Eddie, dun't ask me to do that. I'll be done at 'alf four – let me get 'ome and cleaned up an' I'll come to see thee at 'alf five.'

'OK, fair do's,' said Eddie, 'But don't be late, now.'

Sure enough, at a quarter past five Bruce presented himself at the Kirkby nick and put his side of the story on record on the still new-fangled tape – once Eddie had mastered its operation. He denied assault, claiming that he had acted in self-defence, and named ten witnesses to support him, including one who had seen the incident in the toilet. That man was interviewed and confirmed Bruce's story, while numerous other witnesses came forward to support what had happened in the concert room.

Eddie completed his report and submitted it to his superiors to decide if action should be taken. They deliberated in their own leisurely way, and in the first week of October issued Bruce with a summons to attend the Pontefract Magistrates' Court on 18 October, charged, first, with causing bodily harm to Hedley Salter and, second, with causing a breach of the peace on the same night in the same place. Simultaneously, at the other end of the town PC Eddie and his fresh-faced colleague delivered a summons to Hedley Salter to the same court on the same date for assault against Bruce Johnson, and conduct giving rise to a breach of the peace.

'You fucking lousy bastards!' was how they reported Salter's response. 'I complain, and you fucking summons me! Well, we'll see about this. Fucking Johnson's got it coming.'

'Don't do owt daft, 'Edley,' said PC Eddie, "cos you'll be the first person we'll come looking for. An' for your information, 'e'll be getting a summons for assaulting you about now. If I was you I'd see a solicitor before the eighteenth, because it's a serious charge.'

Bruce came to me on the recommendation of a mutual acquaintance. Usually people choose a solicitor near where they live, but Bruce had done the rounds of the local solicitors with a litter of minor disorder and drunkenness offences, and I suppose he thought going out of the town might change his luck. Hedley, on the other hand, chose the very able services of a local brief, and on 18 October 1984 we all appeared at Pontefract Magistrates' Court, an old building much in need of repair, in which I was a 'foreigner'. Hedley's representative viewed me with suspicion, and sought me out to ask what pleas we would be tendering – he seemed disappointed when I told him we were pleading 'Not guilty'. Bruce and Hedley sat on opposite sides of the room giving each other the dead-eye, and the hostile atmosphere infected the court police officer, who felt obliged, almost like a referee, to warn both the defence solicitors, 'We don't want any trouble in here.'

'Don't worry, we don't plan to fight – at least, not yet,' I replied, smiling at Hedley's solicitor.

'I don't mean you two, I mean the defendants,' said PC Arthurs, a man clearly not gifted with humour.

My opposite number and I went into the court to find the CPS prosecutor, who turned out to be a pleasant but panicky lady in her forties. 'I'm sorry, I can't deal with you at the moment, I've just been given five new prisoner files, and I need to speak to the police officers and check some TICs on another file, then talk to two of my witnesses who've been brought here unnecessarily, and I'm not well, I shouldn't really be at work, but two of my colleagues are already off with stress so I've got to,' she complained, all in one breath. 'Anyway, you won't get on first. There's a big list this morning, and some important matters the clerk will want to call before you,' she added, as if justifying her unhelpful approach. It seemed pointless to reply, so I didn't, whereupon she repeated herself.

'I'm sorry,' I replied, 'I can't speak to you now. I have to consider my client's case and statement, I have to be back in Rotherham for 11.30am, and I've a client outside who's likely to have a fight with his co-accused, and then PC Arthurs will tell me off, claiming that I'm responsible for something I'm entirely irresponsible for, if you see what I mean.'

She looked at me as though I were from outer space and put her spectacles back on – causing the silver chain which secured them to dangle perilously close to her open ink-bottle. 'Allow me,' I said, and pulled the chain safely aside. A 'Thank you' might have been appropriate, but instead I got a blast of vitriol, much to the amusement of the other solicitors on the bench, who I guessed had been similarly treated.

The clerk of the court came out of the Magistrates' Room, and I immediately recognised her as an old friend from another court. 'Good morning, Steve,' she said. 'What case have you got?'

'Johnson and Salter – my friend here represents Salter. We're both pleading not guilty, and the matter is to be sent for trial.'

'Very well,' she said, 'we'll call that first.'

The prosecutor looked at me with hatred as our clients were brought into court. 'I haven't read this file,' she objected, but the court clerk was obviously used to her, and not prepared to be messed about.

'But Mr Smith says they're pleading not guilty, so I see no reason why the plea can't be entered whether you've read it or not.'

'Oh, very well,' said the prosecutor grudgingly, and then the magistrates walked in. The chairman, a lady in her sixties, surveyed the advocates in front of her, fastened her eyes on me, and realised she hadn't seen me before: I could see her thinking, 'Who are you, and what are you doing here in my court?' I sensed a liberal sprinkling of xenophobia, and felt like standing up and volunteering that I'd just come to read the meter. I resisted the urge.

The prosecutor mumbled through her summary, designed to allow the magistrates to decide whether they would deal with the case or send it to the crown court, then my colleague and I both argued that summary trial in the magistrates' court was appropriate. Neither of us went into too much detail, because that outcome seemed inevitable. But in magistrates' court work, nothing is a foregone conclusion. To our surprise, the bench retired to consider their decision, leaving me to reflect on Bruce's statement while they were out.

Bruce's case was that he thought Hedley was going to attack him, and the law doesn't require a defendant to wait until he's assaulted before he defends himself. Then there was a fight, during which Bruce had to defend himself or be given a thrashing. But the prosecution were alleging that Bruce and Hedley had assaulted each other, and breached the peace in the process. One way of dealing with such a case was to bind both protagonists over to keep the peace, a course I'd suggested to the prosecutor. I'd seen her evidence, which wasn't clear on who was guilty of assault, but breach of the peace was implicit in the events in the concert room. It was a straight clash of evidence between Bruce and Hedley, and would come down to whom the court believed.

The bench returned and agreed summary trial. Both defendants pleaded not guilty, but before the case was adjourned, I told the court that a bind-over was on offer. The clerk said that was a good idea if both parties agreed, and invited the prosecutor to comment. Unfortunately she hadn't been listening, and to my surprise said no. The clerk wasn't impressed, and said so. The bench suggested an adjournment so she could consider her position, but she protested that it wasn't in her file, and asked for an adjournment to let the reviewing lawyer make a decision. The case was duly adjourned for a month, and the parties left court.

Following a further court appearance, the CPS agreed to drop all charges if both defendants agreed to be bound over. Bruce was agreeable, but Hedley initially wasn't, because it meant that his assault charge against Bruce would be dropped. However, it turned out that he had other recent convictions, and feared that if he were found guilty of assault he might be sent to prison, so he reluctantly agreed to be bound over, and the charges were dismissed.

But Hedley was still unhappy with the result. As we walked out of the court, he turned to Bruce and said, 'You'll pay for this.'

Over the next few weeks, Bruce slipped back into his old routine: working most days, then jogging in the evenings with his faithful dog Goz – a whippet and Jack Russell cross, a peculiar-looking but affectionate animal that followed him about with complete devotion. On one such run, he was crossing the common when he was spotted by Hedley Salter, who was driving by.

The next night, when Bruce went to Goz's kennel to take him for his evening run, the dog wasn't in its pen, yapping excitedly at the prospect of his daily exercise. He opened the gate to find poor Goz lying lifeless in a corner, a piece of half-eaten meat at his side. Its smell told Bruce what had happened: Goz had been poisoned.

FIVE

JACK'S PIGEON

Allotments are fashionable everywhere now, but in the eighties they were as much a part of northern life as beer, Woodbines and bread and dripping. Apart from providing produce for the dinner table, they gave working men somewhere to develop their hobbies – one of the most popular being racing pigeons, which has a large and fanatical following even today, with participants often spending more time and money on their pigeons than on their families. To rear a champion racing pigeon was a dream of many an allotment holder in Rotherham.

My most consistent clients, the Heptonstalls, had two adjoining allotments, since they'd 'forgotten' to inform the council that Madge's father had died, whereupon his should have been allocated to the next person on the waiting list. Jack had a talent for growing vegetables and breeding racing pigeons as well as thieving, and for a couple of years he and his family had exercised my ingenuity in court less than usual, because they were all preoccupied with Jack's pride and joy, a racing pigeon called Arse – a peculiar name for a pigeon, or indeed for anything. But Jack's Arse was the talk of the pigeon-mad neighbourhood. It had won five races running – or flying, I suppose – the latest being one of the Grand Nationals of the local racing world, the Ingoldmells classic. Jack had had many substantial offers to put him to stud, but turned them all down prior to the 'big one', the race at Fleetwood, which not only offered the winner a handsome prize, but, more importantly, would increase its value substantially. The downside was the risk of kidnap – as Jack told me in shocked tones. So as well as buying a gaggle of geese ('Better than Rottweilers,' he said), he deployed his many sons in a round-the-clock guard roster.

He had often offered to take me on a guided tour of his pigeon loft, but I'd always found suitable excuses. However, in the spring of 1985 I succumbed, and late one Wednesday afternoon was greeted by Jack and three of his sons – the ubiquitous Albert, plus 'our Morris' and 'our Venn', who stood in line like toby jugs, all with the same posture and wide grin. It was my first introduction to 'our Venn', a slightly older version of Albert, with the same straw-like hair and preponderance of gums. 'That's a strange name?' I ventured.

'Aargh,' said Jack. 'It should'a bin Ken, but I 'ad flu when I registered him and the Registrar didn't 'ear me reet. We nivver noticed 'til we got to t'church for the christening, so we just left it at that.' They showed me round both allotments, which were obviously well-tended. The first was abundant with spring crops, from early lettuces and new potatoes to flowering fruit trees and currant bushes; the second housed well-constructed sheds for hens and a fenced area for the geese – which were messy, noisy and very aggressive, taking great exception to my presence. One tried to peck me through the wickerwork fence, but Albert came to my rescue with a few words and a flick of his finger.

'E's gorra way wi' them birds,' said Jack. ''E can make 'em do owt. Watch this.'

Jack turned to Albert, who made a gesture inviting the geese to perform their party tricks. They honked to order, went quiet again at a wave of Albert's hand, then hopped about madly, as if dancing. When the performance ended the family clapped vigorously, and I joined in. Albert then proudly presented me with two large eggs, which he advised me to eat as soon as possible, before they went off. At each stage of the guided tour they gave me samples of the produce, and I filled the boot of my Ford Capri with all manner of home-grown veg before we reached the highlight: the pigeon loft.

Constructed with loving care, this was, in Jack's words, 'fit to live in'. Indeed it was, if you were a pigeon. No expense had been spared in ensuring the comfort of the inhabitants. The whole place was watertight and draught-free, and any self-respecting pigeon would have been proud to perch beneath its portals. There were about thirty of them in all, housed in separate apartments, all warm and cosy. But at the top was one space even more salubrious than the rest – the pigeon equivalent of the penthouse flat. Jack beamed as he proudly introduced me to his prize bird. 'This is my Arse. 'E's t'fastest bird this side o' the Pennines. Tha knows, I'd back 'im against owt. Mind thee, 'e's well looked after – 'e wants for nowt. Good seed, good pellets, rainwater and a bit of Uncle Jack's magic energy pills.'

'Energy pills?' I queried.

'Ah, like a supplement, tha knows… It gi's 'im some oomph.'

'My God,' I thought, 'Jack's drugging the bloody bird!' I'd heard of such things in dog- and horse-racing, but not pigeons.

'Jack,' I said firmly, 'you know it's illegal to use drugs, don't you? What energy pills?'

'Me own formula,' said Jack with great self-satisfaction. 'I mix up some glucose, yeast, and some stuff I get from 'Erbert Micklethwaite. 'E races dogs, and 'e gives 'em energy pills too. Cage gets a bit full, but they'll shift all right.'

'What do you mean, the cage gets a bit full?' I asked.

'Tha knows – wi' shit.'

'Oh,' I said. 'I understand.' I thought I'd leave the subject of the pigeon's bowels and proceed to the practicalities of pigeon racing. 'It's amazing how they know where to fly back to,' I ventured.

Jack and all his boys looked at me pityingly, and Albert, never backward in coming forward – but at least doing his best to hide his smile – said, 'They are called 'oming pigeons, Mr Smith.'

Jack decided it was tactful to change the subject. 'Cast your eyes on this, Mr Smith,' he said, presenting a small container connected to a car battery. He took from it a small polystyrene box and there, encased in cotton wool, was a small blue egg. 'See? That's worth a grand of anybody's money. That, my old cock, is Arse Two.'

'Ah – son of Arse?' I ventured.

'Aargh,' said Jack. 'It's in incubation. I've already 'ad offers for that egg.' He carefully replaced it in its container, then its box, and reconnected the various wires which lay around his bench.

As we left the shed, I noticed a formidable locking and security device. 'You're keen on security, then, Jack?' I asked.

'Certainly am, Mr Smith,' said Jack righteously. 'Tha can't trust anybody round 'ere; they'd 'ave thi fillings aht thee teeth.'

As I walked back to my car, three toby jugs lined up to wave me off, and with a click of his fingers Albert made the geese flap their wings in tribute to my visit. I congratulated Jack on his fine spread, and said that all he needed was running water and a toilet to make the place perfect.

'Argh, we mek do with a bucket in t'shed,' said Jack.

I returned to the office in a mellow mood. All seemed to be going well, although I was putting in a lot of hours and had started to work on Saturday mornings. Jennifer would drive Rebecca to her dancing class, another job I had to delegate, as the business always seemed to come first. – but even that was tolerable, as it was benefiting the business. What awaited me changed my mood considerably.

Over the last couple of years we had been doing a lot of work for a local haulage firm, which had about sixty employees and approximately a million pounds' worth of assets. They had run up a bill with us to the tune of some two thousand pounds, a substantial sum in 1985, especially for a small firm like ours, and Wilf had been trying unsuccessfully to chase them the day before. The morning's post explained why he had had no luck – the company had gone into liquidation, and its assets were much less than its liabilities. There was talk of creditors receiving ten pence in the pound, but when Wilf spoke to the official receiver he couldn't even promise that.

For the first time since we set up in business together, we had to face one of the cruel realities of life. When incurring bills on behalf of clients, we usually asked for money up front, but this firm was one of our major clients, and we hadn't asked for enough to cover our disbursements on their behalf, merely invoiced them for the shortfall on completion. This meant that about a year's work for them had cost us a large chunk of our own money. The directors had fled, and all we could get from the official receivers was a dose of sympathy.

I went to the Rotherham Magistrates' Court that morning with a heavy heart and, for the first time, a substantial business worry around my neck. At the time we had only a tiny overdraft, but this deficit would mean a conversation with our bank manager. He had always come to visit us, but we soon discovered that a bank manager's attitude changes when you are in the red. I didn't sleep that night. Jennifer told me I'd been chuntering, which I put down to too much Guinness as I saw no point in both of us worrying, and at work, my usual buoyant joviality disappeared. The holiday Jennifer and I had planned for later that year had to go, as did the new car, the office-painting scheme, and the spring in my step. We had no experience of putting on a brave face, and I realised that the word 'if' is the most obnoxious in the English language – 'If only we'd…' was a comment Wilford and I often made at first.

But after a week of brooding, I determined to put it to one side, never let it happen again, and fixed a lunch appointment with the bank manager with a view to extending our overdraft. Perhaps fuelled by good wine, the lunch went well, and our credit was good enough for him to extend us an overdraft facility of £20,000 – a huge amount by our standards, and another commitment to be paid out of an already shrinking cake.

As we drank our port – the bank manager's was a double – we were interrupted by a waiter saying that there was an urgent telephone call for me. I excused myself - to hear the custody sergeant at Rotherham police station in fits of laughter.

'Sorry, Mr Smith, but a Mr Jack Heptonstall and his son, who refuses to give his name, request your attendance at the police station. The allegation is theft.'

'Is there something funny?' I asked, none too pleased at having my lunch interrupted.

'Well, I think so,' he said. 'Given the nature of the charge and what they stole… But I'll tell you when you get to the station. Are you coming, or what?'

'What,' I said. 'I'm not finished here. I'll be along in an hour.' And I returned to my guest.

Since I'd agreed to drive that day, I'd limited my drinking to one glass of port, but Wilf and the bank manager had made merry throughout the meal, so it took me a while to force them into my car and drop them off at the Cross Keys for 'a last one' before I could go on to the police station. When I got through the familiar green door to the cell area, it was to discover much hilarity amid the usual chaos. A harassed gentleman was making a statement, with liberal expletives, in the tiny interview room; another man was being violently sick near the breathalyser machine, and a third was screaming down the telephone to his wife, demanding cigarettes and a clean pair of underpants. Sitting in the middle of all this was Sergeant David Brown, who had just come on duty. He had invested twenty-five years of his life in police service and seen it all, or most of it: he surveyed the scene, shrugged, and shook his head with the air of a man close to retirement.

'Excuse me a moment, Mr Smith, if you please,' he said politely, and went about sorting the mess. He turned first to the man on the telephone. 'Would you limit your call to the next ten seconds, please, then return to your cell? I said ten, which is now eight, whereupon the phone will be taken away – conclude it now: no ifs, no buts, no pack drill, just do as I say.'

He turned his attention to the vomiting man. 'PC Withers,' he firmly told his special constable assistant, 'find a shovel and mop, give them to our guest, and tell him to clean it up.' Next, he shouted towards the interview room: 'Hey, you in there, stop bloody shouting and swearing, I'm trying to conduct an effing charge office! If you must effing swear, keep it bloody quiet and at least shut the door!'

Finally he turned to me, smiling politely. 'Good afternoon, Mr Smith, how nice to see you again. How can we help you?'

I couldn't help smiling, and played along. 'May I see Jack Heptonstall and son?'

'Of course. I have a copy of the custody record, which will give you all the details you require.' He looked at it, and smiled. But before he could say anything, his assistant had brought Jack and Albert out of their cell. They both smiled with relief when they saw me.

Jack said, 'They've got me this time, Mr Smith. Bang to rights, I 'ave to admit.'

I was surprised at the sudden burst of honesty, but if he was 'bang to rights', he really had no choice. The arresting officers appeared, ready for the interview, and since there was no argument about guilt, and both Jack and Albert were anxious to return to their allotment, I agreed to start it straight away. As we walked down the corridor to the interview room, Jack said: 'We've got to geroff as soon as we can, because the egg's due to 'atch any time.'

The officers looked perplexed. I got Jack and Albert seated, then spoke to the officers outside. 'What's going on?' I asked. 'Every time I try to talk about this case, everyone bursts out laughing.'

'Well,' said DC Sutton, 'I can explain why. They stole a transportable lavatory – a chemical toilet on a two-wheeled trailer, attached to a vehicle like a caravan. At 8.30 this morning, the said item was parked outside the council offices, for use by the workmen engaged on that site. At approximately 10am it was seen leaving the site, being towed by a Transit van driven by the defendant, Jack, with – we allege – Albert in the passenger seat. The said item was then transported to an allotment on the outskirts of town, owned by the said Jack. Unfortunately for your client, he was seen removing the said item from the site, and within twenty minutes of the theft police officers arrived at the allotment where it was found.'

I asked whether they could prove that it was the same chemical toilet. The officer grinned, and said, 'We have an eyewitness, Mr Smith, not only to the theft, but also to the journey and delivery of the item to the allotment.'

'How?' I asked. 'Did you follow him?'

'No,' he said, biting his lip to try to stop laughing. 'But unfortunately for your client, and indeed for the witness, he was using the lavatory at the time of the theft, and was still present in the trailer when it arrived at the allotment – suffering an acute reaction to a double vindaloo last night... That's the irate gentleman giving a statement to one of my colleagues in the interview room.'

He had done a sterling job of describing the facts with as straight a face as possible, but now the humour of the situation got the better of him. He burst into laughter at the same time as I did, and it was a few minutes before we regained our composure, entered the room and spoke to my clients.

'Did you know someone was using the toilet when you pinched it?' I asked, looking from Jack to Albert and back again. There was no answer, but suddenly my clients' usual huge grins reappeared, and they too burst into uncontrollable fits of laughter. It was some minutes before we were all in a fit state for the interview.

All went well until the police referred to the unfortunate witness, who was found in a state of undress when they arrived. Once again Jack burst into laughter – which infected me, and then the police as well. Mass hilarity broke out – embarrassingly, because Rotherham had recently started to record interviews on tape, which duly recorded a complete farce. Laughter was followed by coughing, followed by a short silence as everyone composed themselves, then more laughter triggered by a further question.

Eventually the interview was completed and Jack admitted his guilt – Albert was exonerated as a mere passenger, and a minor to boot. I waited while Jack was processed for bail, and when they reappeared they were still laughing.

'Why on earth did you steal a chemical toilet?' I asked, once we were outside.

'Does tha' remember when tha came to t'allotments?' said Albert. 'Tha said the only thing we needed was a toilet.'

'Yes, but I didn't mean you to go out and steal one. Especially one with Rotherham Borough Council printed all over it.'

'Ah well,' said Jack, 'We'd just 'ave blanked it out, and tha couldn't 'ave read it. Canst tha gie us a lift? I've no brass for t'bus.'

At the allotment, the toilet had already been towed away by the police, but there was a lot of activity around the pigeon loft. I was turning the car when Jack rushed back to me, shouting, 'Mr Smith, come and see! Come and see!!'

Slightly dubiously, I stopped the car and went in, to find a number of Jack's family surrounding the bench beneath Arse's cage in uncharacteristic silence. I peered down in the incubation box, and saw a crack through the centre of the egg: moments later, I was privy to the birth of Arse Junior, which was quite the ugliest thing I had ever seen.

Jack looked up, his eyes sparkling with pound signs. 'Ain't 'e beautiful?' he sighed.

I looked again, but couldn't possibly agree. It was too private a moment to stay, so I ran the gauntlet of the geese and got back in the car.

As for the interview tapes – the police couldn't destroy them because they were evidence, but fortunately they never had to be played. Except by me, whenever depression rears its ugly head...

SIX

INGROWING TOENAILS AND BRUCE'S REVENGE

The regular Wednesday evening football match was one of the high-lights of my week, though I found it increasingly difficult to get there on time, as long lists of appointments following lengthy appearances in the magistrates' court stretched my working days into the evenings. However, that autumn of 1985 I had major problems with my big toes, for both had been broken in my pursuit of footballing excellence, and ingrowing toenails gave me a great deal of discomfort. When I kicked a heavy ball, the pain was so excruciating that in the end I sought the services of a chiropodist.

My first visit was on a Tuesday morning, the day before the match. I was limping quite badly, with both toes swollen and extremely tender – I even had difficulty pulling on socks, such as was the pain. The waiting room, a museum of 1950s' decor, was lined with photographs and pictures of diseased feet in all shapes and sizes and varying states of decay. The only other patient wait-ing was an enormous woman, with the most offensive left foot I had ever seen propped up on a stool. It was verruca-laden and so red and angry-looking it almost gave off sparks.

'You can go before me, luv, I'm early,' she said obligingly. 'You wouldn't believe I used to be a dancer, would you?'

'No, I wouldn't,' I thought, but I didn't want to cause offence so I just smiled and nodded.

'Just look at my toe,' she invited. 'Then you'll see what real pain is!'

I have never been able to understand people's desire to share their pain with others. 'Yes, I can see it from here,' I said, moving as far away as possible. Luckily, I was rescued by the chiropodist calling me into his consulting room.

The chiropodist was a man of between sixty-five and seventy, with a bowed back, doubtless from years of bending over feet. He was gaunt, with a yellowish complexion and extremely long, thin fingers, but the most disturbing things about him were his bottle-bottom glasses, which didn't seem to help him as much as they should have. He kept bumping into things and knocking them over, each time making the weary comment, 'Oh deary, deary me.'

He motioned me to sit on his consulting chair, which had a stool in front of it, and take off my shoes and socks. He cleaned his glasses, replaced them, and again invited me to sit down.

'I am sitting down,' I said, surprised.

'Oh, of course you are, splendid. Now then, what can I do for you, madam?'

All confidence in him vanished. In my deepest voice, I said, 'It's my two big toes. I have ingrowing toenails in both, and I'm in a terrific amount of pain.'

'Oh deary, deary me,' he replied. 'Ingrowing toenails can be very nasty, and if they go septic it can lead to all sorts of problems. You do remember the story of Douglas Bader, the fighter pilot, don't you?'

I certainly did, given that the story had led to Lidster's nickname, and I didn't appreciate the reminder.

'Let's have a look and see what we can do,' he continued, removing his glasses and staring at my feet, which I had rested on the stool. As he fumbled towards me, he knocked my right big toe and, once I was off the ceiling and back in the chair, decided to examine the offending toes with his fingers. I shot back to the ceiling, and reminded him that I was in considerable pain.

'Well you would be,' said the chiropodist. 'Ingrowing toenails can be extremely painful.' For some reason the word 'arsehole' sprang to mind. I'm not usually squeamish, but my anguish was so intense that I suggested there might be some way of freezing the foot to eliminate some of the pain.

'What a good idea,' he said, reaching out for some spray, and coated my foot with wasp killer before finding a soothing anaesthetic spray. In an instant I was completely numb from the knees down, and protected against marauding wasps to boot. He then set about his work with relish. I thought I saw blood at one stage, but by the time I plucked up the courage to look more closely he had mopped up whatever I had lost. Finally, he appeared to have finished.

'Thank God!' I thought, but my relief was short-lived. 'Right, now I'll do your other foot,' said my tormentor.

'Oh Christ!' I replied, staring up at the ceiling in readiness for my next visit.

Despite the anti-freeze dispensed about my lower limbs, the pain was still intense, and I began to sweat profusely.

'Oh deary, deary me, this little bugger is being awkward,' said the old man.

'He certainly is,' I replied, referring to another little bugger, and visualising him in a Gestapo officer's uniform.

After what seemed like an eternity of torture, he stood up in triumph, holding a piece of bloodstained nail with a pair of tweezers. 'Got him!' he exclaimed. 'I think you'll find that your problems are over for the time being. But I'm afraid they will grow back the same way; you'll need the treatment again. How do you feel now?' asked the chiropodist.

'I haven't felt like this since the Spanish Inquisition,' I replied sarcastically.

'Splendid,' said my torturer, oblivious to sarcasm.

I attempted to move, but the magic spray had not worn off. As I tried to stand my legs gave way and I fell, landing on the plastic container which housed the day's collection of other people's toe-nails, verrucas and dead skin. All dignity gone, I staggered to my feet again and wobbled out like a drunk, to be greeted by the woman with the rotting foot.

'Did it hurt, love?' she asked.

'Not at all,' I said, wiping sweat from my face and neck. The lady then hobbled into the consulting room. As I tottered down the stairs, I could have sworn I heard her hit the ceiling.

By the time I got back to the office, the effects of the magic spray had worn off and my toes were throbbing mercilessly. I limped into reception, where Wilf was opening the post.

'You're hobbling like an old man,' he commented.

'I've just had my toes done,' I replied, seeking sympathy, as our cleaner Mrs Mott joined us.

'He's limping like an old man,' Wilf told her.

'Terrible thing, that gout,' said Mrs Mott. Since she had given up smoking at New Year (with heroic determination, since she'd chain-smoked all her adult life), she had compensated by increas-ing her prophesies of doom and supply of old wives' remedies. 'Makes you limp like an old man. My father had it, it killed him, you know, killed him dead.'

'Gout can't kill,' I said.

'It did him. He tried to cross the road, but he was too slow. A lorry ran him over! If it hadn't been for the gout, he'd have got out of the way... So you want to watch that. It's a killer, gout is. Cup of tea, Mr Smith?'

'Yes, please,' I replied, nodding my head.

'Have you any anti-gout pills?' asked Wilf.

'No, but I've got some senna pods. They'll clear your system out,' replied Mrs Mott. 'That's what you need, a proper clearout.'

'It's only ingrowing toenails, Mrs Mott,' I protested to her dis-appearing back. 'Marvellous,' I announced. 'Now she'll tell the bloody world I've got gout, and that she's recommended a good clearout. I hope she doesn't tell Pagey.'

'Killed her father, that,' said Wilf solemnly.

'Bugger off,' I replied, and limped into my room, my bid for sympathy having fallen on stony ground.

I had various letters to answer, and quite a bit of junk mail to lob into the waste bin. It was a little contest I had with myself each morning. I was fairly accurate, but that day I failed on all three throws, a bad omen.

As I was busy dictating to my secretary Sheila, the telephone rang. 'Pontefract police on the line for you,' announced Tracy. 'Sounds urgent.'

'Hello, Steve Smith speaking.'

'Good afternoon, Mr Smith. Sergeant Tindall, Pontefract police. I'm ringing to see if you can help us. I understand that you act for Bruce Johnson of South Kirkby?'

'I did,' I replied, 'but his case finished nearly a year ago.'

'Well, he might be contacting you. We've been looking for him, and he knows it. The night before last, near a South Kirkby public house, a man called Hedley Salter was involved in a fight. He was knocked unconscious, and died on his way to hospital. We believe your client Bruce Johnson was responsible, and we're anxious to interview him.'

I felt irrationally guilty, as though the police thought I was concealing something. 'I'm afraid I can't help, Sergeant. He may have made other arrangements and seen someone else. But if he contacts me, I'll certainly be prepared to advise him,' I said forcefully.

'I hope you'll get him to hand himself in. We wouldn't want you to stick your neck out, would we?'

'No, we wouldn't,' I said, refusing to grab the bait, and put the telephone down, thinking what an offensive sod the sergeant was. But I couldn't help thinking about Bruce too. What if he had killed Hedley?

The rest of the day passed quickly. I saw a long list of clients, and it was almost 6pm before I finished. It was very quiet, and by the time I'd packed my briefcase with a few files, turned out the lights and locked the doors, there was no one else about – yet I had a feeling I was being watched. The office looked out over a small green in front of the churchyard, with bushes lining the path to the church, which was pleasant during the day, but quite eerie at night.

The bushes rustled in the breeze, and a voice said, 'Mr Smith?' and again, 'Mr Smith?'

I looked around, saw no one, and began to walk towards the sound. 'Who's that?' I asked.

'It's me, Bruce Johnson, from Kirkby. Look, I need to speak to you, urgent like, but they're looking for me. Is your office empty? If it is, you go in and I'll follow. Just for a few minutes, please?'

'OK, Bruce,' I said, turning back to the office door. 'Everyone's gone.'

I stepped inside, and almost immediately Bruce was there. He was dirty, his clothes looked slept in, and he glanced from side to side as if expecting to be discovered at any second: every inch a man on the run. 'The police are looking for me,' he said breathlessly.

'I know,' I replied as I led the way upstairs. 'They rang me this afternoon, thinking you might have contacted me. I told them I hadn't seen you.'

'I'm sorry,' said Bruce. 'I shouldn't have come, but I didn't know where to turn.'

'What happened?' I asked, once we were settled in my office.

'Well, you know Hedley never forgave me for getting off that court case, and he poisoned Goz. It was an 'orrible thing to do; that dog never hurt anyone. Well, all this time I've just kept out of his way, but on Monday night I ran into him outside the local, so I challenged him about it. He went for me, and I defended myself. I only hit him once, honest, but he went down – it wasn't natural, it was as if he was out before he went down. I tried to pick him up, but he was out, so I propped him up and buggered off. Then I heard he'd died, an' I panicked and ran off. I've borrowed a mate's car, 'cos the police know my registration number, and I've just driven around, lying low during the day. They're trying to get me for murder!' Bruce, the fearless man's man, was trembling, a terrified creature, like a rat in a trap. 'What do I do?' he asked.

There was really only one reply I could make. 'You've got to hand yourself in – it won't look good if they have to fetch you. Then we prepare our case. I don't think you'll get bail, but there's always a chance.'

'Oh aye, one in a million,' said Bruce derisively. 'I might get out of the country.'

'They'll be watching every port and airport. You won't get out, and it'll make you look guilty,' I pointed out.

Bruce thought about that. 'But they won't believe me,' he objected.

'Why not?' I asked. 'Are you sure you only hit him once? You know they can make forensic checks?'

'I'm sure. And it wasn't even a punch, I didn't really connect.'

'Then why not tell the police just that?'

Bruce wouldn't answer. He was right to look on the black side, but he needed to be realistic: in this instance there was only one thing to do, which was to give himself up and explain what had happened.

'Will you come with me?' he asked, when I eventually persuaded him of this.

'Of course, and stay for the interview. The first thing we'll need to know about is the post mortem – that's the medical examination of the body to find the cause of death. When they do that, we can get our own opinions too.' To reinforce what I'd already said, I went on: 'Stay on the run and sooner or later they'll get you and want to know why you didn't hand yourself in. They'll think you've got something to hide. But according to you, you acted in self-defence, and you say there's no witness to dispute that,' I repeated his defence case.

'They'll put me inside. I just can't stand the thought of prison.' At that, the big man started to cry. I've seen many so-called hard men fold up like a pack of cards at the mention of prison, for few people enter those gates gladly.

But when Bruce regained his composure, he accepted it. 'Okay, I'll give myself up, but I've something I need to do first.'

'Well, I have to go to court in the morning, but I'll be finished about noon. How about I meet you at Pontefract police station at quarter to one? I'll ring the police in the morning and tell them you're coming in.'

'You will come, won't you?' asked Bruce pathetically.

'Yes,' I replied, 'but don't have me on a wild-goose chase. I'll see you at a quarter to one – and don't say anything to the police until I arrive.'

Bruce nodded in grim acceptance, and set off into the night.

The next day I went to court early, hoping to finish promptly, but my luck was out. One client, Terry Truclove, failed to attend, and the court issued a bench warrant (for him to be detained in custody until the next available court). But, true to form, he turned up late, ruining my morning.

'They've issued a bench warrant,' I told him.

'Sorry, Steve, but I overlaid,' said Mr Truelove, a man of few words, with a harelip and shocking wind. He liked a drink, but difficulties with his digestive tract meant that a big 'session', as he called it, played havoc with everyone else. Terry was light-fingered, and had visited Silverwood Colliery's stack with a number of strong plastic sacks to fill – he had a number of customers eager for cheap fuel, no questions asked, who kept him in beer money.

There was a queue to get cases on, and the magistrates had

retired to consider another case, so I and several other solicitors were cooling our heels on 'waiting time', which caused more stress than the job itself. We all fingered our watches nervously, as if waiting for the VAT man to call.

The bell rang from the Magistrates' Retiring Room, which meant that they required the clerk's assistance. That day it was Geoff Clarke, with whom I had an understanding: he was very experienced, and I used to take him my queries when I wasn't sure of the law or what to do. 'Hurry them up, Mr Clarke,' I pleaded. 'I've got to be in Pontefract by 1pm.'

'You shouldn't take so much on,' said Clarkey. 'Pontefract's not your area.'

'I know, but it's a murder,' I said, in the hope of some sympathy.

'You can't rush a bench,' said Geoff, 'murder or no murder.' Which of course was right, but didn't help me.

Eventually, I left the court at 12.30 pm, which gave me fifteen minutes to travel the fifteen miles or so to Pontefract. For part of the way I seemed to be following an endless queue of heavy lorries, plus one Danish sightseer who didn't know how to get his hire car out of second gear, so I arrived at Pontefract police station at 1.05pm in a state of high stress – only to find an empty waiting room. Either the police had taken Bruce into custody, or he hadn't turned up.

I rang the bell on the counter, and after a minute or so the office door opened and a large and very butch policewoman with bulging biceps and a slight moustache appeared at the desk. 'Yes?' she demanded, in an intimidating growl.

'I'm Steve Smith, solicitor from Rotherham, and I have an appointment with my client Bruce Johnson, to be interviewed in relation to a murder allegation.'

That caught her by surprise. 'Murder?' she asked.

'Yes, murder,' I said, and smiled.

'Sit down and I'll check,' she snarled, and left the room with a sigh, making me feel guilty for bothering her.

A couple of minutes later she returned. 'You're late,' she said curtly. 'Well, sit down. They'll be with you in a minute; they're booking your client in now.'

Unfortunately, for some reason the police officers needed for the interview weren't available, so I could either sit and wait in Pontefract ad infinitum, or go back to the office to clear other work. I chose the latter, and Bruce understood perfectly, simply asking me to fetch him a copy of the *Sun* while he waited.

Back at the office I dealt with a list of messages, then ventured into the waiting room to see Tracy wearing her latest creation, a purple mini-skirt with purple boots and a peculiar cap. Tracy looked good in anything, but you never really knew when to take her seriously.

'That's an unusual colour, Tracy,' I admired. 'The purple of your skirt and top.'

'It's not purple,' she said. 'It's Moldavian blue.'

'Oh,' I replied. 'Are there any more messages for me?'

'Yes,' said Tracy. 'There are two sticking out of the red diary.'

'Do you mean the Lithuanian pink one?' I asked, smiling.

'No, the red one,' said Tracy, 'with the messages sticking out.'

At 5.25 pm, just before the phones were switched off, Pontefract police called to say that Bruce would be interviewed at 5.45 pm, which left me twenty minutes to get there. I set off straight away, but again got stuck behind what I'm convinced were the same lorries that had hindered my trip earlier in the day, and eventually arrived at 6pm to find that the police had gone off for their evening break. When they returned, there was a preliminary interview with Bruce, who stuck to the same story he'd given me. It only lasted a matter of minutes, and was adjourned pending the results of the autopsy. I then travelled the short distance to Pontefract Hospital, while Bruce remained in custody.

It isn't unusual in murder cases for the defence to commission an independent pathologist's report. Sometimes one can arrange for the defence pathologist to prepare this in conjunction with the prosecution expert, as in this case we could, because the autopsy had been delayed for some reason. I had instructed Professor Mike Gilchrist from Bradford to act for us – luckily he was available. Professor Gilchrist had an excellent reputation; I had worked with him before, and was happy to work with him again.

He entered the waiting room with a spring in his step, a tall man of about sixty, with a shock of grey hair and the air of a mad professor but who, despite his rather grisly job, retained a youthful look. Extremely intense and devoted to his profession, he embarked on his duty with a vigour that shook most of us with queasier stomachs. I suppose that as a medical man he was used to seeing all life's frailties and complications, but for some reason he enjoyed it.

Professor Gilchrist stared at me through bright blue eyes over his horn-rimmed glasses before saying, 'Well, I've made a cursory inspection of the deceased, but I can see no exterior signs of injury that would have caused death, so I'm going to consider the question of the heart, and also the brain. You can be present during the autopsy if you wish.'

I gulped, and the coroner's officer looked at me with a grin which meant 'Have you got the bottle for this, old boy?' I decided to wait outside.

The autopsy took about an hour, and at the end of it the professor came back to the waiting room, his green smock blood-splattered.

'You'll be pleased to know it's an aneurysm, resulting from the weakening of the artery wall due to a variety of possible causes. Loss of elasticity and contractibility due to a deficiency in the media is the most important factor.'

I looked at him as though he was speaking Greek. He continued:

'Sometimes the arteries at the base of the brain develop a weakness in their walls as a result of natural disease. When the blood is pumped through them, and especially if the blood pressure is raised, these defects cause a progressive weakening of the wall, and the artery develops an aneurysm, rather like a bubble in bubble gum. Once it has formed, one of two things can happen. Firstly, blood may form a clot within the aneurysm, so that the defect is sealed up within the lining of the blood vessel, which virtually restores the normal flow of blood. However, if this compensatory mechanism does not take place the aneurysm is at risk of rupturing, causing a massive haemorrhage. Death may result immediately from this catastrophe, or be delayed for a variable period of time.

'One of the factors which may cause the aneurysm to burst is a sudden increase in blood pressure, as a result of a burst of physical or emotional activity. On the other hand, a rupture may occur at any time, even if the person is at rest or asleep. The legal aspect of causation can be complex in these cases. It could be argued that the physical and emotional outburst generated by the confrontation could have raised the blood pressure, which precipitated the fatal outcome without a single blow being struck. On the other hand, knowing that the rupture could have happened at any time would make it impossible to prove beyond doubt that the alleged assault had anything to do with the death.'

The professor looked at me for a reaction. I took the bull by the horns and asked, 'What do you mean, exactly?'

He repeated every word, a little more slowly than before.

'Oh,' I said thoughtfully. 'In fact what you're really saying is that he died of – er...?' I looked at him for inspiration, and his expression made it clear that he had realised he was dealing with a complete imbecile.

'Brain haemorrhage,' he said briskly. 'A congenital defect of the media in the angles formed by the junctions of vessels. In other words, particularly with hypertension, this area of weak artery is breached and blood leaks out of it into the skull, causing death.'

I was a little happier with that, and proceeded to ask some more imbecilic questions. 'Could a blow to the head have caused it?' I started.

'Possibly, but I rather suspect that in this case, since there were no significant exterior injuries to the head, it was simply a case of a brain haemorrhage. Looking at the condition of the brain, it could have happened at any time: the deceased, I am afraid to say, was living on borrowed time. It is my opinion, and that of the professor representing the police, that your client's conduct did not contribute to the death. Looks like you're on to a winner this time, Mr Smith,' the professor concluded.

'Looks like it,' I said, 'but you never know. Well, thank you, Professor, I'm most grateful. You'll send me your bill?'

'Yes, of course. 'Bye for now, then, until the next one.'

It often seems strange that professionals deal with death in such a matter-of-fact way, but someone has to do it. My job can be bad enough, but dealing with autopsies is something else.

The police, disappointed that the medical evidence proved their first impressions and suspicions wrong, were still keen to interview Bruce, but not before I had told him the news. I saw him in a poky Victorian cell, no more than ten feet by six feet, in the Pontefract police station. It was antiquated and chilly, stank of stale body odour and vomit, and the only furniture was a wooden bed, its frame covered with names carved into the surface.

I put him out of his misery straight away. 'You didn't kill him, Bruce,' I said. 'It was a brain haemorrhage, and the pathologist seems to think that you did nothing to contribute to the cause of death.'

Bruce slumped back on the wooden bed, and it was as if five years disappeared from his brow in an instant. All he could say was, 'Thank God! You said a brain haemorrhage?'

'Yes. An aneurysm, actually, a result of the weakening of the artery wall due to a variety of causes. Loss of elasticity and contractibility due to a deficiency in the media is the most important factor,' I said, implying expert knowledge.

'Eh?' said Bruce, implying that he hadn't a clue what I was on about. He paused, then spoke again. 'I didn't want him to die, I really didn't… What'll happen to me now?'

'They want to interview you, just to have your account on paper,' I said. 'And then I rather suspect you'll be released. You may be charged with a breach of the peace, but I doubt it, as it doesn't seem you actually offended anybody at the time. If they do charge you, my advice is to refuse to answer any questions.'

I made this decision because the police had nothing to dispute Bruce's account of the incident, so would be left with no option but to release him, so to keep tight-lipped was the best advice I could give him at the time. Whether it was morally right or wrong was not a consideration: my duty was to represent him to the best of my ability.

When the interview began, the officers ignored the forensic and autopsy evidence, and behaved as though their careers depended on securing a confession from Bruce. I had to interrupt on at least three occasions when I thought they were overstepping the mark, until they finally saw that there was no new ground for them. However, Bruce did admit that there had been an incident and an exchange of words, which the police thought sufficient to charge him with breach of the peace. This in turn placed him in breach of his bind-over from the earlier occasion, so gave the police something for their efforts. He was to go before the court the next morning, which gave me severe difficulties. As well as having cases in Rotherham, I had one for an old client in Barnsley. I toyed with the idea of doing Pontefract first, then back to Rotherham and across to Barnsley, but that was a forlorn hope. Thankfully an old mate dug me out of the proverbial in Barnsley, and I decided I'd have to deal with the Pontefract matter first and then travel to Rotherham.

When I arrived at Pontefract there was a queue to get on. The court clerk had got out of the wrong side of the bed that morning and was particularly unhelpful, while the prosecutor was one who seemed to make a point of not reading my files. I managed to get back to Rotherham by noon, having secured bail for Bruce, to be greeted by the emphysemic usher, smoking his beloved Capstan full-strength. 'You're in for it this morning, Steve. The court's been retired for twenty minutes waiting for you.'

'Haven't they got any other work to do?' I asked.

'No, the trial finished early and they split the work up, so everyone was finished by about half eleven.'

'Bloody marvellous,' I thought. I wouldn't have minded the Grade Four bollocking but for the fact that I was just trying to do a day's work, not skiving or enjoying myself. I put on my tin hat and armour-plated vest and went to face the music, and was grateful that the magistrates seemed sympathetic. The clients were less so.

'I suppose tha stopped in bed this morning?' said one of the whingers.

'Yes,' I said. 'I was drunk last night and decided I'd stop in bed, and I feel much better for it, thank you.' The speed of my repartee left him for dead, but as I went to deal with another client, I heard the words 'idle bastard' floating down the litter-strewn corridor.

My list finished just before 1 pm, and back at the office there was a telephone call from Bruce Johnson. I thought it was nice of him to ring to thank me for my efforts, but I was disappointed.

'Is that you, Steve?' said Bruce.

'Yes, it is. How are you now?' I asked.

'Better for being out of that bloody hole,' said Bruce. 'I'll tell you why I'm ringing. I want to know when I can have my trainers back, the police kept them.'

'You'll have to wait until you see what happens about the charges, Bruce. If they take no action, of course you're entitled to them back. If they continue with the proceedings, then you should get them at the end of the case.'

'Do you think I'm going to get done, then?' said Bruce. 'For this breach of the peace lark?'

'Well,' I said, 'Who can tell? The police have to have something on their books – after all, a chap died.'

'Ah, but that wasn't my fault, he was dying anyway. I just wish he hadn't poisoned me dog.'

'Yes, well, I think he's paid the ultimate penalty, don't you?'

'Goz was still my dog,' said Bruce. 'Right, well, I'll let you know if I'm done or not.' And then all I could hear was the dialling tone.

'Thank you very much indeed, Mr Smith, for your sterling work and efforts, for inconveniencing yourself so greatly over the past two or three days running round at my beck and call, missing meals, creating ulcers and receiving bollockings from magistrates,' I said aloud to myself, just as Sheila came in.

'Are you talking to yourself, Mr Smith?'

'Yes,' I said. 'I'm just being grateful on someone's behalf.'

'Oh, that's nice of you,' said Sheila, picked up the file she was looking for and disappeared.

I turned to look out of the window at the churchyard, and remembered the words of my old boss George Tierney: 'If you expect thanks in this game, you'll be disappointed. If it's thanks you're after, join the Salvation Army.'

Just before the next hearing of Bruce's case, the charge against him was dropped. I wrote to him with the good news, pointing out that he could collect his trainers from the Pontefract police station. I didn't receive a reply.

SEVEN

THE SINS OF THE FATHER

I first met Marie Pearson in 1985, when she had been charged with grievous bodily harm. Marie had become an unmarried mother in 1964, when she was just sixteen: she had known the father for just two weeks when Gaynor was conceived, and loved him because he looked like Paul McCartney – the new pop group The Beatles was then all the rage. Sadly the relationship didn't last as long as 'She Loves You' was in the Top Ten, and by the time Marie missed her second period he had left the area.

Marie lived with her parents until she got fed up with them trying to run her life, then found a bedsit and left Gaynor with childminders while she went out to work. Soon after Gaynor started school, Marie met Kevin, an unemployed labourer who, after a few weeks, suggested they set up home together. They moved into a council house and put the rent book in their joint names – the only real commitment Kevin would ever make to the relationship. A bully and a drunkard, he took out his dissatisfaction with life on Marie and her child; Gaynor soon learnt to hide in her bedroom when her stepfather came home drunk, so as not to be the focal point of yet another argument. Nevertheless, she would often lie on her bed in tears with her pillow over her ears, trying to block out the sounds of her mother being beaten.

On a 'dole day' evening that August, subjected to yet another beating, Marie finally snapped. She took the poker from the fireplace and struck back, so hard that Kevin was knocked out, with serious bleeding and a hairline fracture of the skull. The emergency services managed to save his life, and while he was being treated in Rotherham Hospital, Marie was interviewed by the police.

They afforded her every courtesy, and even assistance, during the interview, so that her case could be placed in the best possible light. She was bailed immediately it was over and allowed to go home to her children (by now she had twin boys by Kevin, as well as Gaynor). From her statement, I got the impression that the police, having had considerable dealings with this bully over the years, felt Marie had given him no more than he deserved. Sometimes it's unfortunate that the law can't look at things that way too. On that occasion, I advised Marie to plead guilty, despite the serious nature of the assault. She did, and was placed on probation for three years, which was probably the best course.

Less than a year later, Sheila brought my post into the office – the usual mish-mash of begging letters from the prison and circulars offering complete solutions to my financial and emotional needs. 'There's a good offer on cellulite reduction, two treatments for the price of one,' she said helpfully. 'And do you remember that horrible case about the woman who was bullied by her husband?'

'Which one? There are so many,' I sighed.

'It was Marie Pearson, and she and Gaynor are in reception, wanting a quick word. She seems upset, so I've told her you'll see her.'

'Oh thank you, Sheila,' I said. 'And is there anything else I can do for you while I'm at it – clean your car or hoover your stairs, or perhaps a bit of ironing?'

Sheila looked at me reproachfully, so I sighed again and capitulated. 'All right, show them in.'

Marie was pretty well dragged in by Gaynor, who watched intently as her mother told me she had finally decided it was time to have Kevin thrown out of her home. He had made many promises to mend his ways, she said, but always broke them as soon as he got drunk.

Marie had clearly suffered a great deal. Apart from the violence, the physical signs of which included surgical scars to a badly damaged top lip and an arthritic left hand, the years of unhappiness and abuse had dulled her personality, destroyed whatever confidence she had had, and made her think she might be to blame for Kevin's behaviour. She assured me that there had been good times, and there were the twins to think about: his conduct towards them had not been nearly as bad as towards Gaynor.

At this Gaynor tutted fiercely and shook her head, her hatred of her stepfather written all over her face.

'Have you ever got on with him, Gaynor?' I asked.

'No,' she said. 'He's a drunken offensive pig and a coward. My mother's had to put up with his nasty behaviour, his beatings, and worst of all, he's taken away her identity.' And Marie couldn't find it in herself to argue.

'What are we going to do about it?' I asked, trying to direct the conversation away from Marie's humiliation.

'Can you help us?' Marie asked. 'Can we do it so I don't have to be in the house? Because if he knows we've been here, we'll be for it.'

'We'll have to issue proceedings, and they'll have to be served upon him,' I said. 'Have you anywhere else to stay until we get the matter before the court?'

'I could stay with my sister,' said Marie, 'but she's got no room for the kids. Where would Gaynor and the boys go?'

'Don't worry about me,' snapped Gaynor. 'I've told you before, I'm eighteen, I can take care of myself. And we'll find somewhere for the boys.'

'How old are they?' I asked.

'Fourteen,' said Gaynor.

'How do they get on with their father?' I queried.

'Very well, really,' said Marie, brightening up.

'No they don't,' said Gaynor. 'They're scared stiff of him, and well you know it.'

Marie gave no answer: I've seldom felt sorrier for a fellow human being.

'I'll complete all the necessary papers, and then I'll need to see you in a day or so to take a full statement. Will you come and see me on Friday?'

'Of course she will,' Gaynor answered for her. 'I'll see she's here,' and with that they left. Marie walked with a slight stoop, her coat had seen better days, her shoes were down-at-heel, and her perm in the final phase of its lifespan. She looked like what she was – a downtrodden and abused woman. But at least Gaynor's air of defiance made it quite clear that she wasn't going to follow in her mother's footsteps.

On Friday, Gaynor arrived on time, but Marie wasn't with her. 'Where is she?' I asked.

'I thought she'd be here. I've not come from home – she *said* she'd be here...'

After a while we both realised she wasn't coming. I really felt for Gaynor, and for a moment was unsure what to say. 'Perhaps she's been delayed... missed her bus, even... a number of things...'

My excuses fell on stony ground. Finally, trying to be positive, I said, 'I'll keep the papers handy, and see to it when she's ready.'

Gaynor didn't say a word, but just shot me a resigned half-smile, thanked me for my help and left.

The following day I was walking through the town centre when I noticed a familiar woman walking towards me – although a black eye and swollen mouth disguised the face somewhat. Our eyes met for a second, but Marie looked away, pretending not to have seen me. About a week later I met Gaynor, who said she had finally left home and rented a one-bedroom flat just out of town. She had no intention of returning home even for a visit, but still expressed concern about her mother.

As soon as I left the office the following Friday I dismissed any thoughts of work, as that weekend was to be our second trip of the year to the Lake District. Since discovering that beautiful area a couple of years earlier I'd got hooked on the place, particularly Bowness on Windermere, and when work permitted Wilf and I would take our wives for weekends away from it all.

Initially, much of our time was taken up sightseeing and seeking out the best hotels, restaurants and pubs. However, on our last few visits we had found ourselves looking at 'For Sale' boards, and even stopping to look in estate agents' windows on the way to our favourite pubs...

Wilf couldn't make that particular trip, so Jennifer and I invited Christopher Good and his wife Pat to join us. Goody and I had been friends since we had met at the nursery school in South Kirkby, where my father had been a butcher at the Co-op, and Chris's parents had been the licensees of the local working men's club. On the Saturday afternoon, he and I went for a stroll via a couple of pubs before reaching Hayton & Winkley, estate agent, which had a number of properties displayed in the window, including Number 4 Priory Cottages, Windermere. For some reason it caught my eye, and before I even realised I'd formulated the idea, I dragged Goody back to the hotel to get the car, and we were on our way to view it.

It was well hidden behind a hotel called the Priory, which had been built in the shape of a medieval priory by a local eccentric in the late nineteenth century, but we finally found it. As we drove down the track, we saw two rows of cottages, one further up the slope than the other to allow both a splendid view of the lake. In front of them was a large open lawn, and a parking area with two spaces for each cottage. It looked perfect.

We parked, and after a quick look at the outside of Number 4 took a small, winding path through two fields to the water's edge and a recently built landing-stage, about a third of the way down the lake from Windermere itself, towards Ambleside. I was totally captivated in an instant, and we drove back to the estate agent for more information, the keys and a conducted viewing. We got all three, and by the time we returned to our wives at the hotel my mind was made up.

The cottage certainly needed repairs and redecoration; it was cold and damp, and some time in the recent past a major pipe had clearly burst. The front door opened into a cottagey lounge and kitchenette area, which in turn led to a narrow hall off which were a bathroom, complete with shower, and two bedrooms, one of which was only big enough for bunk beds or a single. It was very small, but quaint, and I believed the potential was fantastic.

That night we dined in the lovely Old England Hotel in the centre of town, which had managed to retain its 'olde worlde' atmosphere despite being bought by one of the big chains. As we ate in the dining room, which overlooked a small lawn, a swimming pool, and the lake beyond, I talked endlessly about the potential of the cottage. Jennifer and the Goods were left in absolutely no doubt that I believed it had to be mine.

On Monday I returned to work and told Wilf of my exploits, and he agreed to go with me the following weekend to see 'our cottage'. His reaction was the same as mine, so the first thing we did the next Monday was see our friend and accountant Michael Jarvis to discuss how we could acquire it. Michael checked it out, and told us he thought it had great investment potential – which was spot on: some years later, it saved us from bankruptcy. We put in an offer, which was accepted by return, and within four weeks Wilf completed the sale. We had become property owners in the Lake District! It was yet another financial commitment, but I felt that no sacrifice was too great for this particular venture. Our weekends became devoted to cleaning the place up, with my parents co-opted to help with the painting and decorating. I was determined that the cottage would be ready for the following Easter, and nothing would stand in my way.

On the first Monday in September, I had a large court list beckoning. At that time I had no one with whom to share my court work – Wilf worked on the conveyancing side of the business – and was finding it increasingly difficult to satisfy our ever-growing client list. I surveyed the court diary for that morning, and rang the cells to see if there were any new prisoners I was unaware of. They told me I had three, but the names hadn't been put on the board and all they could tell me was that they were male.

I turned up early to try to be ready for a 10am start, and steal a march on my other colleagues in the list. I saw Cyril Jackson first, a local ne'er-do-well who showed all the signs of becoming a regular client. Unfortunately, there was little I could do for him, because he faced two charges of burglary and a number of TICs, had a long list of previous convictions, and had failed to comply with a community service order. He decided, quite sensibly, that there was no point trying for an adjournment; he knew he was going to prison, and felt that the sooner he got there the sooner he would get out.

The chairman of the magistrates was a tweed-suited spinster of considerable experience but short on sympathy. 'Cyril Jackson, you will go to prison for three months,' she said. 'Take him down, please.'

'You old cow!' shouted the disappointed defendant.

'What did your client say?' asked the magistrate, peering over her horn-rimmed glasses.

I thought very quickly. 'I think he was expressing regret at his sentence, madam,' I said.

The chairman turned first to the colleague on her left, then the one on her right, for confirmation of what had been said. Whether either had heard Cyril's choice phrase I can't say, but it wasn't repeated, and my plight was relieved by the magistrate's clerk calling on the next case.

At that point the usher tapped me on the shoulder, coughing his germs along the solicitors' bench, and told me that two unnamed clients wanted to speak with me immediately. It's annoying, having fought to get your cases called as soon as possible, to be dragged out of the queue and lose your place for something inconsequential, such as to see if you have a light, a packet of cigarettes or the bus fare home. 'I've only just got to the front of the queue. What the bloody hell do they want?' I asked.

The usher didn't know, and indeed I shouldn't have expected him to: he was doing me a favour even by passing on the message. Coughing into my ear, he said, 'They say it could be a matter of life and death.'

'It could be a matter of life and death for them, if I lose my place,' I said irritably. 'Tell them to go and get a cup of tea, and I'll join them in the tea room as soon as possible.'

The usher kindly went to pass on the message, but it was only a matter of moments before he returned. 'Mr Smith,' he said, 'they ask if you have any change for the tea.'

With a groan, I reached into my pocket and brought out a pound coin, which I handed to the usher, who walked off smiling and coughing.

'Next case, Mr Smith,' said the clerk to the justices, as the defendant was brought in. 'Are you Michael Wellington McIver of 2 Lansdown Crescent, Eastwood, Rotherham?' he asked.

'Yes, miss,' said my client Spider (otherwise known as Mr McIver), the boy with tattoos all over his face, who seemed to be having trouble with his eyesight.

The lady chairman peered over her spectacles at him with displeasure, and asked, 'Are those tattoos all over that young man's face, Mr Smith?'

I could hardly say 'Isn't it obvious?' so I just replied, 'I'm afraid so, madam.'

She turned to one of her colleagues, and the words 'disgraceful sight' were just about audible. At least I think she said 'sight', though I could have been mistaken. Either word would have been appropriate.

Spider had been caught in possession of amphetamine sulphate, popularly known as speed. He had been in a poor state even before he discovered drugs, but his condition had worsened as the addiction gripped him, leaving his face grey and drawn, and he sniffed repeatedly, a telltale sign of cocaine abuse. He had only recently been released from serving a sentence for possession with intent to supply, and was already at it again. The charge this time was simple possession, but he was still in a serious position, and the court would be looking for a return to custody. As he was pleading guilty, his case would be adjourned to enable probation reports to be prepared, and maybe the Probation Service could suggest a way to deal with him which didn't involve another 'free holiday'. My application for reports was granted immediately, but the magistrates made it clear that they were considering remandment in custody pending them. We were given a date to return to court for sentencing, and Spider was given his bail form. I told him to wait in the corridor until I completed my next case, which I did as quickly as possible, then left the relatively clear atmosphere of the courtroom for the putrescent public corridor, a veritable rogues' gallery of peering eyes watching every move of the court users.

My 'life and death' visitors were none other than Jack and Albert Heptonstall. They were sitting quietly in the WRVS tea room, and when I entered they both stood to attention, which suggested they were really worried about something.

'What's up, Jack?' I asked.

Before he could answer, we were interrupted by a fellow with long, black, greasy hair and a mouthful of black teeth framed by chapped lips. His suit seemed to have welded itself to his body, and his face hadn't seen soap, water or a razor for many days; his eyes were bloodshot, and he peered constantly from side to side, as if expecting a visit from a debt collector at any moment. He spoke with a Scottish accent in a low, secretive tone, punctuated by regular helpings of the f-word.

'I've a fecking charge; jest a wee problem, deception, OK? It's a plain no' guilty plea; there's nae evidence, so they'll have to let me off, an' if they dinna I'll appeal. I'm gaeing back hame to Scotland for three months, and I want it adjourning until I fecking come back. There shouldn't be any fecking problem wi' that, should there?' His question sounded more like a statement.

'Oh, it's as simple as that, is it?' I replied sarcastically.

'Aye,' came the reply. 'It fecking is.'

At that point the usher approached and wheezed, 'They're calling one of your cases in Court Number 2, Steve.'

'Right. I'll be back in two minutes, Jack, I've just got to see what Court Number 2 wants.'

'Whit about me?' our Scots friend interrupted.

'I'll see you in two minutes too. Just let me sort this out,' I said. Then the jailer appeared, and told me they'd brought in another prisoner who had to go to hospital, and needed to see me straight away.

As I ran to Court Number 2, I felt a tug at the back of my coat. 'Lend's a quid for a cuppa tea, Steve,' said my assailant.

'Sorry, pal, no change,' I replied, which found no favour, though for once it was true. 'That's what they all say,' he said sulkily, just as I was told someone wanted to speak with me on the telephone in the cell area.

I stood quietly and counted to ten to avoid a stroke. I was back on track and about to enter Court Number 2 when the hem on my jacket was yanked again. Turning, I was confronted by an unfamiliar face issuing a torrent of garbled words and spluttered crumbs from a bun he was trying to eat. 'The coppers've done me, reet, and I ain't done it, reet, an' I'm not having it, reet? So it's a not guilty plea, reet? I've been dragged here on this spoonest charge.'

'Do you mean spurious?' I asked.

'Aye, spoonest, and I'm not 'aving it, reet?' He thrust into my hand a set of summonses which had apparently been used as place mats in a Chinese restaurant. The charges related to not having a television licence, for which he wouldn't be able to get legal aid – yet he was berating me as though I'd issued the summons myself. But I kept my composure, and refrained from kneeing him in the groin. I handed back his summonses with the tips of my thumb and forefinger, and said I'd speak to him as soon as possible. He continued to shout his disquiet into the space behind me as I entered the solemnity of Court Number 2.

The magistrates were reading a probation report, but looked up on hearing the commotion to see who the infiltrator was, and I got the distinct impression that they were unfairly blaming me for the noise. The usher intervened, escorting the importunate man back to the reception area, the word 'reet' ringing through the court corridor as he went. I dealt with my case, took a deep breath, and re-entered the court corridor, dodging the spillages of WRVS coffee and the feet of one of the town drunks, who was strung across the corridor singing an off-key version of 'Edelweiss'.

I finally got Jack and Albert into the 'rat-hole' interview room. 'Tha looks 'arassed, Steve,' said Jack.

If you admit to being harassed you can give the impression you're too busy, which sometimes puts clients off, so I chose my words carefully. 'Not really, Jack,' I said. 'Nothing I can't handle. What's to do, then?'

'Coppers 'ave got our Morris, and they're going to interview him. Tha knows what Morris is like. 'E'll admit to owt when his knackers are squeezed.'

'I don't think the CID will do that,' I said.

'Tha knows what I mean,' said Jack. 'It's an expression, like. Can tha ring 'em? I don't want him interviewed wi'out tha's there.'

I reassured him; they left, and I raced into Court Number 1 to regain my place. The rest of the morning went reasonably well. The man with the bun went away satisfied after we arrived at a suitable arrangement with the prosecutor, and the Scotsman was nowhere to be found: I suspected he had adjourned his own case.

When I got to the police station, the custody sergeant confirmed that they were not squeezing Morris's knackers, but had released him without charge. I immediately phoned Jack, who thanked me enthusiastically, saying that I was the 'best thing since sliced bread'. I told him I'd done nothing, but Jack's reply said it all: 'Ah, but tha were there, weren't thee? Tha turned up and he got out. Thanks, Steve, I'll buy thee a bottle of whisky for tha' trouble.'

That conversation typified one of the many peculiarities of my profession. If the defendant gets a good result, whether through your skills or not, you get the credit. But when a defendant gets what he believes is a bad result – usually because he's offended and deserves it – the solicitor often gets the blame. I've heard many defendants say things like, 'I don't like him, he got me three years,' when referring to their solicitor or barrister.

I got back to the office just before 2pm, to find an urgent message to go to the hospital to see Marie Pearson: apparently Kevin had beaten her up good and proper this time. There was also yet another client clutching a large wad of summonses, but I side-stepped him, went into my office and picked up the telephone. I got through to the hospital straight away, and discovered that Marie was in casualty. Apparently she had been subjected to a violent attack which had left her with multiple cuts and bruises and, more seriously, a depressed fracture of her right cheek; she had also lost three of her front teeth.

I arranged to visit her later, then set about dealing with my many afternoon appointments – a mixed bag, including two divorces, one lack of a TV licence, two burglars and a relic from the hippy era, who had been done 'for smoking happy fags, man'. At 6pm I arrived at the hospital, and was shown into a side ward. Gaynor was sitting by the bed, holding her mother's hand. I was shocked to see Marie in such a dreadful condition. Both her eyes were badly swollen and had started to bruise; her right cheek was clearly depressed, and her lips were stitched and swollen. There were scratches all over her face and neck, and I could see thumb-prints around her throat. She was clearly in acute discomfort and cried when she tried to speak.

'Don't, Mother,' said Gaynor, also tearful. 'It'll be all right.'

I didn't need to be told how Marie had come by her injuries, and certainly not who had inflicted them, but was interested to know if the police had been involved.

'No,' snapped Gaynor. 'They weren't told, so he's got away with it again. They arrived at the same time as the ambulance, but she wouldn't make a complaint. One day...' she said, her voice tailing off.

Marie was in such pain that I asked as few questions as possible. Gaynor chipped in with other details. It seemed that Kevin had come home drunk and found that some money he'd put aside for cigarettes had been spent on bread, whereupon he lost his temper and hit her about the face. When she could take no more and fell to the floor, he kicked her in the stomach and then grabbed her throat. It was only when she went limp in his hands that he realised he had gone too far, and fortunately for Marie, she only blacked out momentarily. Had the assault continued, she could well have been taken to a mortuary rather than a hospital.

'My mother wants to take this to court, Mr Smith, and this time she will turn up. Isn't that right, Mother?' Gaynor looked at Marie, who nodded in grim acceptance; she knew she had no alternative.

I just made out the words, 'He nearly killed me,' before I asked her to rest while I completed my notes.

It was a week before Marie could leave the hospital, during which time I prepared the documents and had them served. Kevin had made no attempt to see her, or even find out how she was getting on: surely, in those circumstances, Marie would go through with the case? With the hearing just four days away, I invited her to the office to ensure that she wouldn't change her mind. Marie kept the appointment, looking much better, and still adamant that she was going through with the court action for a personal protection order against her common-law husband. On the day Kevin did not attend, and the application went through on the nod.

Next day Spider was back for sentencing – as the luck of the draw dictated, before the same magistrate who had adjourned his case for reports four weeks earlier, when she had been unimpressed by either Spider's personality or the tattoos all over his face – and who could blame her? But the probation officer had a lot of sympathy for Spider, and I felt he got it absolutely right when he said that Mr McIver had been a victim of others much more devious than he, who pretended to be his friends, and had become their unwitting tool. He recommended that Spider be placed in a probation hostel well away from the area for twelve months, and abide by their rules and regulations. This seemed appropriate in Spider's case, because just about everything else had been tried, including prison, which had achieved absolutely nothing except a further burden on the taxpayer's purse. Prison is necessary to protect the public from dangerous offenders, but is sometimes misused because the courts don't know how to deal with offenders who aren't a threat and sometimes because they're afraid of looking 'soft' – neither of which helps anyone.

As Spider and I left the rat-hole, Jack was waiting in the corridor. 'What's to do, Jack?' I asked.

'Aye oop, Steve,' said Jack, ''ave tha gorra minute? I need to ask your advice about something. Like, what would you do if you were me? Tha sees, it's like this, Steve; I've got t'chance of a job.'

'You've what?' I looked at him incredulously. He was fifty, and had never worked for anyone in his life. 'A job? Do you mean working for a living?'

'Aye,' said Jack, 'Tha sees, me and Madge have been thinking, and thought it might be a good idea, like.'

'Bloody hell, Jack,' I said. 'Steady on. It's a bit extreme, isn't it? What is it?'

'There's this bloke, tha sees, he's reet wealthy, and his passion is pigeons. Well, he's fancied my Arse for ages, and offered me four grand for him. That's a lot of money. So I've sold 'im Arse, an' now 'e's asked me to look after his racing lofts.'

I couldn't believe that the pigeon world had a millionaire-backed racing loft, but clearly it did.

''E says 'e'd gimme a good wage, an' we can live on his farm in caravans. We went last week to 'ave a look. It's reet neece, an' t'kids think it's great – all but our Albert. It's a long way from his mates, tha sees, and 'e dun't want to move.'

'Where is it, Jack?' I asked.

'Geordie land, up Northumberland way,' said Jack. 'On a farm near t'coast. 'E's wanting to breed pigeons, an' 'e's going to put my Arse to stud.'

'When will you have to go?' I asked.

Jack paused to reflect. 'End of the year,' he said. 'It's a bit sudden like, but he wants to get on wi' it, an' 'e's arst me to move up by Christmas. These millionaires are a bit pushy, tha knows.'

'But you'll have to give up your council house,' I suggested.

'Aye,' said Jack, 'That's t'problem. But I'm getting too old to keep getting into trouble, and it'll be a nice new start for Madge 'n t'kids. An' anyroad, I've nivver 'ad a job.'

I looked at him and properly assessed him for the first time: a man who had lived a fairly uncomplicated life, bringing up nine children in near-poverty and adversity. Most people would dismiss him as a common criminal, and technically they'd be right, but in his own way he had a sense of honour and a strong moral code. He never compromised me, was always a delight to act for, and I'm not ashamed to say that I liked him; he was charming, except in the matter of other people's property. As he described his new-found job, I saw excitement and pride on his face. This was to be his first job at fifty, doing something he was good at. Perhaps it would be the making of him.

'Well, we'll certainly miss you and the kids, Jack – even that bugger Albert,' I said, smiling.

Jack just laughed his singular laugh and shrugged, before taking a deep breath to ask: 'Does tha think I'm doing reet? Tha sees, it's a big risk, giving up our 'ome an' all, but I just feel I've got to 'ave a go.'

'If you feel like that, Jack, have a go. If you don't, you'll always wonder whether or not it would have worked out. Of course it's a risk, but sometimes in life you've no option but to take them. But this is a question only you and the family can answer. I wouldn't like to point you in any direction, but I just hope you won't have any regrets either way.'

'I see what tha means,' said Jack. 'I might kick mesen if I don't try.' He stood up and held out his hand, which I shook firmly. 'Ta for everything. I 'ope we'll see thee before we go. Tha can come down for tha dinner wun neet.'

As soon as I got back to the office, I found Wilf and told him Jack's news.

'Does that mean that little sod Albert won't be bothering us again?' he asked.

'Yes, I suppose it does,' I said. On the other hand, I reflected, it also meant losing our best clients.

Exactly a week later, I was driving to work listening to Radio

Sheffield when I heard a report that a woman was to appear in court charged with attempted murder.

I was shocked when she was named as Marie Pearson. When I arrived at Rotherham court later that morning I found that Marie had seen another solicitor, but Gaynor was waiting anxiously to see me, trembling and beside herself with worry.

'I need to speak to you, Mr Smith,' she said.

'Of course, come with me,' I said, and took her to the rat-hole.

'It's my mother. I think she's admitted trying to kill him,' she blurted out.

'Just wait a moment,' I said. 'Try and calm down, and tell me exactly what happened.'

'You see it was all about me, it's my fault. There was an argument at home, and my mum lost her temper, but it was all my fault.' Gaynor started to cry.

'Look, wait a minute. I'll get you some tea.' I went to the WRVS canteen and collected two cups of coffee-coloured tea, but by the time I got back to the rat-hole Gaynor had gone. However, a little later in the morning I saw Marie being brought in, handcuffed to two burly female officers. Although it wasn't my case, I stood at the back of the court and listened as the prosecutor made his application for a remand in custody.

His opening related that, on the night in question, a drunken Kevin had forced his way, unannounced and uninvited, into the council house and found Gaynor making one of her rare visits. At the sight of her Kevin lost his temper, and there was an argument. He struck Gaynor, and also Marie when she tried to interfere, but when he put his hands around Gaynor's throat, Marie picked up a pair of scissors and stabbed him repeatedly. She then telephoned the emergency services, and an ambulance came, followed by the Rotherham police. The prosecutor read out the fact that Kevin was in a critical condition on a life-support machine: it was likely that he would die from his injuries.

I spotted Gaynor sitting at the back of the court to my right, wringing her hands nervously as Marie's solicitor asked for bail. But as this was a very serious allegation, Marie was remanded in custody to Her Majesty's Prison at Risley, near Warrington. Gaynor was distraught. She stood up and ran to the door, and as she brushed past me I heard her mutter, 'It's all my fault, it's all my fault!'

On Thursday I was down at the police station to interview one of my clients, who had stolen fifty recently planted conifers from a newly built bungalow on the outskirts of Rotherham. As I was waiting, Gaynor walked into the station, and I asked how her 'step-father' was.

'The last I heard,' she said, 'he was still very ill, but that was a couple of days ago.'

'And your mum?' I asked.

'She's okay – much stronger than I ever thought she would be. I see her every other day and she writes every day. She's been fantastic, really. She's settled in well, and she says the other prisoners respect her because she stood up to a bully.' Gaynor sounded quite bright, but there was no doubt that she was finding it hard to come to terms with her mother's predicament; she was much more withdrawn than her usual defiant self.

As I chatted to her, two officers appeared in the doorway, one of them a detective inspector, who said very formally: 'Gaynor Pearson, I have to inform you that there's been a development in the case of the wounding of your stepfather. The good news is that he has regained consciousness and the hospital staff are confident he will make a full recovery, although it may be some time before he will be fit to be discharged.'

Gaynor breathed a sigh of relief, but the DI went on: 'I now have to inform you that we have had the opportunity of interviewing Mr Kevin Kelly, and heard his account of what happened on the night in question. On the basis of that information, Gaynor Pearson, I arrest you on suspicion of attempting to murder Kevin Kelly on the eighteenth of this month. You are not obliged to say anything unless you wish to do so, but whatever you say will be taken down and used in evidence.'

I held my breath. Gaynor simply bowed her head, and said, 'It was all my fault.'

Before she was taken away, I told the police I was her solicitor. The inspector asked Gaynor if she wished me to be with her when she was interviewed. She nodded, and we were led into the cell area.

EIGHT

THE SINS OF THE MOTHER

Gaynor was taken to the charge office and booked in, then placed in a cell. The detective inspector took me to one side to explain the latest developments.

'To be frank, we were always a bit suspicious about this case, so we decided to leave our enquiries until Kevin regained consciousness. Fortunately for everyone, he did so,' said the inspector gravely. 'He told us that he came home and found Gaynor on her own. He asked her what she was doing in the house, and she gave him a mouthful. There was a violent argument, and she stabbed him – simple as that.'

I didn't think it was as simple as that: something didn't make sense. 'I think there's more to this than meets the eye,' I said. 'But if you can give me ten minutes with Gaynor, I'd like to speak to her before she's interviewed.'

There was no interview room free, so I had to go into a cell, a small, stark room with walls plastered in graffiti, a strong smell of bleach, and only a wooden bench to sit on. Gaynor was brought in, and sat on the bench next to me. I had considerable sympathy for her, and asked her to tell me the full story.

Gaynor's eyes narrowed as she began. She had gone to see her mother when she knew her 'stepfather' would be out, but arrived before her mother got home and was surprised by Kevin, returning early. Primed with a mixture of drink and the desire to dominate the hated Gaynor, Kevin had grabbed her and tried to impose himself on her. Gaynor spurned his advances and was trying to fight him off when Marie arrived. Horrified at what was happening, Marie tried to interfere, but Kevin thumped her and she fell to the floor; he then gave Gaynor two powerful blows to her face.

Knowing she didn't have the physical strength to stop what she feared was going to happen, Gaynor looked around for something to hit him with. The first thing she saw was the scissors. She seized them, and stabbed Kevin repeatedly in the back until he slumped to the floor.

The two women had sat in silence, gripped by the enormity of what Gaynor had done, clinging to each other for what seemed an eternity before Marie took charge and phoned the emergency services. The ambulance arrived together with the Rotherham police, to find the two blood-spattered women still huddled together by the telephone.

Kevin was taken to hospital at once, and another paramedic stayed to treat Gaynor, who was also injured and in shock, with both her eyes swollen and her nose bleeding from the thunderous blows Kevin had given her. The police questioned Marie while this was happening, and she volunteered a confession before Gaynor could speak.

Both women were then taken to the hospital for further checks, where Gaynor was admitted with shock and suspected concussion. She was kept in for three days, during which she hardly spoke to anyone. In the meanwhile, Marie had already been charged with attempted murder and remanded to Risley Prison.

Gaynor stopped speaking, and I sat back on the bench, surprised by the revelations. 'But you know you'll be charged with it now,' I said.

'Not quite,' said Gaynor. 'I'm not going to say anything to the police unless they promise to release Mum and take no action against her. She was as upset as me, and didn't know what she was saying.'

'I don't think the police can guarantee that,' I said.

'Well,' said Gaynor, 'if they can't, I can't guarantee to speak to them.'

At that moment, a policewoman came in to say they were ready to interview her. I stood up, forgetting I'd put my fountain pen on my lap, and it fell. With lightning speed, Gaynor stretched out her left hand and caught it before it hit the concrete floor.

'Hey, I'm impressed. That was one of the quickest moves I've seen in a long time,' I said.

'I play a lot of badminton,' said Gaynor. 'It's sharpened up my reactions.'

In the interview room, the police clearly sympathised with the women, but stressed that they couldn't give Gaynor any guarantee about what would happen to her mother, as that might be construed as offering an inducement. But Gaynor was open with them, taking care to absolve her mother. She claimed vociferously that she had acted in self-defence, although it was a moot point if using scissors in that way amounted to self-defence.

Afterwards, the police contacted the Crown Prosecution Service and arranged for Marie to be returned to court for the magistrates to reconsider bail. Against the odds, I was successful in my application, although the conditions imposed were extremely tough – they included a curfew, an order to have no contact with Kevin, and another to report to the police station daily at a specified time. The police had been good enough to let me have copies of the medical statements, together with detailed photographs of Kevin's injuries. My problem was how to confirm what had really happened, as there were now three versions of the incident.

By a strange coincidence, that evening I attended a lecture at the Medico-Legal Centre in Sheffield, where one of the speakers, a specialist in forensic medicine, gave a fascinating talk about how one could judge how wounds had been inflicted by studying medical reports, detailed photographs and the weapons. During the coffee break, I asked him about stab wounds, which led us into a brief discussion of Gaynor's case. I showed him the medical report and the photographs in my briefcase.

He made a startling discovery. According to him, of the six wounds sustained by Kevin, the photographs and report confirmed that four had been inflicted by someone using their right hand, and the remaining two by the left hand. He said that he thought at some stage during the attack the assailant must have switched the weapon from one hand to the other, though he couldn't say at what stage.

I remembered seeing Marie's arthritic left hand in my office, and Gaynor's reaction in the cells when I dropped my pen and she caught it left-handed. A disturbing picture began to form in my mind.

'Could another explanation be that the right-handed wounds were inflicted by one person and the left-handed wounds by another?' I asked.

'That would certainly be a possibility,' he replied.

I thanked him, and went to claim my free coffee and biscuits with a good deal to think about.

The next day was a Saturday, and I had to attend the morning court on behalf of three prisoners – one persistent shoplifter with whom the police had lost patience and were asking the court to remand in custody; the second, the town drunk who'd been arrested for the fifth time that week; and the third, an unfortunate burglar who had broken into a scrapyard to steal 'a bit of stainless' and fallen foul of the owner's Rottweiler, who had bitten his bottom as he tried to escape over the wall. The list was finished by 11.00 am, with the shoplifter free to carry on shoplifting, the drunk to carry on drinking, and the burglar going home to rest on his front.

On Monday, the formalities of Gaynor's case were quickly dealt with, and a date before the end of the year was arranged for the trial at Sheffield. Given the different stories Marie and Gaynor had told the police, separate counsel had to be instructed for each defendant. It was a bizarre case. I was used to dealing with two defendants who blamed each other, but it was unusual to have two co-accused blaming themselves and absolving each other.

The prosecution had a man seriously injured by stab wounds inflicted by one weapon: someone had done it, and it was for the jury to decide who that person was. But surprisingly, there was no forensic evidence – because Marie had admitted the charge immediately, the police thought there'd be no need to go to the expense of detailed forensic testing. It was only when Kevin regained consciousness that another version of the incident came to light – but Kevin's evidence wasn't reliable, since he was drunk at the time (his blood had been tested when he arrived at hospital, and found to be four times over the legal limit). He also admitted that he couldn't remember certain parts of the incident.

Gaynor claimed self-defence, saying that Kevin had been selective in his memory, and the part he couldn't recall was his vicious attack on her. As the defence of self-defence insists that a person is only entitled to use proportionate force to that being used against them, the jury had to decide three things. They had to decide: firstly, who had inflicted the wounds; secondly, whether it was fair to use scissors when the attacker was not so armed; and finally, if they felt the number of stabs was excessive.

My arguments were: firstly, the prosecution had to prove beyond reasonable doubt who had caused the wounds; secondly, Kevin was a big, powerful man, over six feet tall and weighing seventeen stone, with a history of violence, so a woman would have to take extreme measures to defend herself against him; thirdly, if the jury accepted the last point, how many blows were excessive if the defendant believed there was a real prospect of one or both women being killed? I hoped for a sympathy vote from the jury, but in a case such as this anything could happen – and in the event, it did.

On the first day of the trial both Gaynor and Marie were ter-rified. If they needed to learn any lesson, they had certainly learnt it during the waiting period leading up to the trial. Marie was determined to take as much of the responsibility as possible, for she said she had less to lose, but Gaynor wanted to protect her mother, so the result was a stalemate.

By this time Kevin had fully recovered. Apart from one visit to the house with the police to collect his belongings, there had been no contact between him and Marie and Gaynor since the incident; he had left the area and was living with a sister somewhere near Manchester. By 10.45am he had not appeared at court, and the prosecuting counsel asked the police to find him. The case was adjourned until 12 noon to allow for that and at noon was put back until 2pm. We were then surprised to be told that Kevin was aware of the hearing, but had chosen to take a day trip to Calais to buy some duty-free booze for his forthcoming wedding celebrations. It was my belief he had deliberately kept quiet so that Marie and Gaynor would have to suffer the long, uncertain wait at court.

Kevin had not endeared himself to the prosecution, nor to any-one else for that matter. My opposite number at the CPS told me there were warrants outstanding for his arrest for non-payment of fines, and a matter of failing to appear at the Manchester Magistrates' Court for police assault. 'It seems that the com-plainant has skipped the country and won't be returning in the foreseeable future,' he said.

'Well, it looks to me as though you're up a creek without a paddle,' I suggested. 'How are you going to prove your case now? There's nothing to counter the defendants' evidence.'

'But how do you explain the wounds?' he asked.

'How do you?' I countered. 'What does it matter, anyway, a rotten shit like that!'

'Is that what we have to tell the judge?' he asked.

'Why not?' I replied. 'You can leave out the word "rotten".'

He laughed, and went to discuss the situation with his counsel. If we had been talking about a black eye or a broken nose I suppose there wouldn't have been much difficulty, but as we were dealing with serious injuries it remained to be seen if the judge would sanction a dismissal of the charges.

I went in search of Gaynor and Marie and found them downstairs, just outside the tearoom. I persuaded them to have some tea, but they declined the bacon sandwiches I brought with it. Waste not, want not, I thought, and tucked in. As I feasted, I noticed a marked silence between mother and daughter. I didn't expect them to be particularly talkative, but it became obvious that they were waiting for me to finish eating, so as soon as I had, I asked, 'Apart from being here, is there something else troubling you?'

At first there was no reply, then Marie said, 'There's something about our case we need to tell...'

Just then we were interrupted by her counsel, requiring an urgent word. I made my apologies to Marie and walked off with him to a nearby interview room. The news he gave me was a massive relief, but I had done this job for too long to pass on such information until it was confirmed: there's nothing worse than building up hopes only to dash them later. I waited in the courtroom for him to return from seeing the judge, avoiding Marie and Gaynor and the earth-shattering news they wanted to impart.

Within five minutes all three counsels returned from the judge's chambers with the thumbs-up sign, meaning that the prosecution had decided not to proceed. However, the matter would 'lie on the file' rather than be dismissed. Neither Marie nor Gaynor had been acquitted by the jury, so couldn't claim a not-guilty verdict, but it was a good enough result for them, and for the opposing counsels there was honour on all sides.

My CPS colleague approached me and said, 'It wasn't really

worth bothering with. It seems that when the complainant was told he wouldn't be able to claim criminal injuries compensation, he thought, "Sod it", but decided to make sure your clients would go through the mill first. The judge said he wouldn't object to the course suggested – which means that he thought our complainant was probably a rotten shit!'

I set off to see Gaynor before anyone else could. She and Marie were sitting where I'd left them, holding hands. I couldn't help feeling sorry for them, but this was going to be no kick in the teeth.

'Gaynor, can I have a quick word? Marie, your solicitor will be coming in a moment, but he won't mind if I tell you...'

'Steve,' said Marie solemnly, 'it was...'

Just then the investigating detective inspector walked past, and I hastily interrupted Marie in my turn. 'It was three bacon sandwiches and tea, I think you were going to say, is that right?' I said, ushering them into the tearoom, and as soon as the officer was out of earshot, I blurted out the news.

Both ladies hugged each other and me, and then the tears came. I left them alone in a quiet part of the tearoom while I ordered the sandwiches.

'Are these all for you?' asked the lady canteen assistant in a gruff, gravelly voice.

'Probably!' I replied, looking back at two extremely relieved ladies. 'Yes, probably...'

After the usual long-drawn-out rigmarole of choices, I delivered the tea and sandwiches. The tea was taken readily, and this time, much to my disappointment, so were the sandwiches. As I sat down Gaynor reached for my hand, squeezed it and just said, 'Thank you.'

'Yes,' I said, 'they're bloody good sandwiches, aren't they? You're not going to eat all of them, are you?'

Both mother and daughter laughed, thinking I was joking. They were anxious to leave, but now there was to be no trial I wanted to know what they had been going to tell me earlier.

'Well,' said Marie, ignoring Gaynor's obvious reluctance, 'we wanted to tell you who actually…'

Just then Peter Baker QC appeared, wanting to speak to me about the case.

Gaynor seized the opportunity, took her mother's arm, said farewell and left, leaving me to be treated to two bacon sandwiches by my learned colleague, who then left me to pay for them.

On my way out of the courts I bumped into Gordon Trousdale, a court clerk and a good friend. 'Good result, Smithy?' he queried.

'Certainly was,' I answered.

'Fancy a quick bacon sandwich?' he continued.

'Just had five,' I replied.

'Good old Smithy,' said Gordon, 'ever the wag,' and walked off laughing.

As I drove back to Rotherham, I couldn't help wondering who had done what – but did it really matter in the great scheme of things? At least it was a satisfactory end to an unsatisfactory case.

NINE

BYE BYE, ALBERT, JACK, MADGE, MORRIS, BORIS, CLORIS & VENN, ETC, ETC

A week before Christmas 1986 was the day the Heptonstalls were moving north, so I paid one last visit to Jack's house to wave them off. When I arrived, there was all manner of transport waiting to carry them off to Northumberland – Jack's and Morris's Transit vans, plus various other vehicles driven by some curious people I hadn't seen before. With all the traffic, I had to park some way down the street, and walked up to the house just in time to see Albert's menagerie being carried onto a vast removal van with the words 'Ray's Removals' painted, less than professionally, on the side. I stood and watched as three dogs, two cats, seventeen racing pigeons and a large pig were carried on board, followed by a burly man with a huge beer belly and a snake around his neck, who struggled down the garden path and into the van, not to be seen again.

Next came a long-haired youth dressed in biker's leathers, with a steel ring through the side of his nose, carrying a gorilla's head and a rather limp blow-up doll. After him came someone with a full suit of armour and a mounted moose head bristling with antlers, then Jack, with a large cardboard box full of cigars.

'Eh up, Steve,' said Jack. 'It's reet decent of thee to turn 'aht to see us afore we go.'

'That's all right, Jack. I was in the area so I thought I'd just say goodbye.'

The whole street had turned out, almost as if it was some kind of party, and many of the neighbours pitched in with carrying duties as the procession of unusual *objets d'art* appeared and then disappeared into the waiting vans.

'You have some very unusual antiques there, Jack,' I said.

'Aye,' said Jack, 'I've been collecting 'em for years, tha knows. We were going to 'ave a shop but we nivver got round to't.'

'Where's Albert?' I said.

''E's abaht somewhere,' said Jack. 'He wants to see thee before 'e goes. We've got thee a present. It's a bit of a surprise, really, but tha's been good to me family over the years, an' we thought you might like something special to remember us by.'

I couldn't help thinking that I had plenty by which to remember this family; after all, I had built my practice on Jack's patronage. But it was a wonderful thought and a splendid gesture, and I was deeply touched by their thoughtfulness.

As Jack and I were talking, Madge appeared, carrying a very heavy-looking box. 'Canst tha manage that, Madge?' said Jack.

'Not really,' said Madge. 'It's a bit too hivvy for me.'

'Well, do tha best then, lass,' said Jack, turning back to me. 'She's a good strong lass, our Madge. O'course as she's got older, tha knows, she's not as fit as she wor, but she can lift like a gud'un.'

Madge was certainly doing much more lifting than Jack, but then Jack always said he liked to 'share it out a bit'.

He invited me into the house, which was empty apart from the carpets and a telephone on the floor in the corner. 'We're leaving 'em that phone,' said Jack.

'You're generous to a fault, Jack,' I said noting that the telephone belonged to British Telecom.

'Does tha know, Steve,' said Jack, 'I was born in this 'ouse. Aye, an' our Morris too, an' our Venn.'

'What about Albert?' I asked.

'Nay, at the 'ospital, our Albert was. Madge 'ad a bit of trouble wi' 'im.'

'Get away,' I said, accepting every word. 'He's certainly run true to form ever since, hasn't he?'

'Aye,' said Jack. 'But 'e's a good lad. I don't 'ave favourites, but if I 'ad I think it'd be 'im. I just wish 'e were 'appier about moving. 'E's a funny lad, our Albert.'

'There's certainly nobody quite like him,' I agreed. 'He's a character and a half, and I've got to like him.'

'Aye,' said Jack, 'everybody does. There's no 'arm in 'im really, tha' knows. 'E's a bit deep and keeps things to 'issen, but 'is 'eart's in t'reet place, 'e's reet loyal, and 'e'd do owt for thee. Aye, an' t'rest on us would an' all.'

I smiled, a bit embarrassed as I realised that it was quite a solemn occasion for Jack, leaving the home he had lived in for all his fifty years. 'I really hope it works out for you, Jack,' I said.

'Well, Steve,' said Jack, 'it's a job, and I'm going to do it the best I can, and the lads will be reet too.'

'I think you should, Jack. There's nobody can work with pigeons quite like you.'

'Only our Albert. 'E's a genius wi' animals, tha knows,' noted Jack, looking round his house for the last time. We walked outside to find his brood were all in a line, and I shook hands with them one by one, ending with Madge just as Albert appeared. The usual cheeky grin was conspicuously absent as he walked up to make a solemn presentation.

'Steve, tha's not like a solicitor,' he said, which I didn't know whether to take as a compliment or not, 'an' tha's always treated us with respect. Solicitors've always got them gold watches on chains in their weskits, an' we noticed tha 'asn't got one, like proper solicitors 'ave, so we've got thee this,' said Albert, thrusting something into my hands. 'It's engraved an' all,' he assured me. 'Every time tha looks at this, tha'll think of us. We'll part as mates.' And he held out his hand for me to shake.

All of a sudden I felt very humble, moved by Albert's speech. All the same, I looked for chewing gum hiding between his fingers, ready to be deposited on me, one of his favourite party tricks. But his hands were spotlessly clean, and there was even a fine parting in his hair where he'd wetted it down. I realised with a slight shock that the person I still thought of as an irrepressible imp – or limb of Satan, depending on what he was up to – had been growing up without me noticing. I thought back: he must be fifteen by now. For a moment I felt very old.

Before I could reply, or open the present, Albert said, 'I've got to go now. If tha's ivver up in our neck of the woods, tha can come and stop in one of our caravans.'

I found myself accepting his offer, and indeed could hardly suppress the lump in my throat as the wagon train moved off, with Albert waving from the back of the removal van. And I was quite overcome that they had taken the time, effort and money to buy a present for me.

I opened the box and found a hunter watch with a chain, like 'proper solicitors' wear, then opened up the watch to read the inscription. Squinting at the backplate in the winter sun, I could just make it out: 'To Frank for fifty years with British Rail.'

'ALBERT!' I shouted, but to no avail. The wagon train had disappeared over the brow of a hill, taking Jack and Madge Heptonstall and the kids to a new world.

I looked at the watch distrustfully, having visions of my career going up in smoke if I became a receiver of stolen goods. There was a slip of paper I hadn't noticed before sticking out of the box, which I opened out of curiosity – and breathed a sigh of relief. It was a receipt from a second-hand jeweller, endorsed with Albert's name. The gift was bona fide, even if it had given me a nasty scare for a moment. Which, when I thought about it, was rather a good metaphor for the Heptonstall family...

TEN

ALL FOR LOVE

It was a magnificent spring morning. The smell of freshly-mown grass pervaded the warm air, courtesy of a local council workman who perpetually broke the speed limit for lawnmowers so as to finish his shift early. I had taken a day off to deal with weighty matters at home, namely planting my tomatoes in the greenhouse, a job I enjoyed because it offered a bit of peace in an otherwise stressful world. It was such a beautiful day that I set up a table out on the patio to admire the view, and began work with relish.

My parents were staying with us at the time, and apart from the garden, one of my mother's favourite pastimes was cooking (a great relief to Jennifer, who often found it a chore). At lunchtime she came out with a tray and set before me a feast of fried gammon, eggs and tomatoes, a real delicacy. I put the plants aside hungrily.

'Have you washed your hands?' snapped Mother. I hadn't, and was almost dragged off by the ear, like a recalcitrant schoolboy, into the washroom to carry out her orders. When she was satisfied, I went back to the greenhouse and tucked in. There's something very special about fried gammon, egg and tomatoes, especially if taken with an extra-large mug of sweet tea. The salt in the fry-up enhances the sweetness of the tea, but a second cup is never quite as good.

I eked out the tea until the end of the meal, then cut up the gammon rind, put it on the bird table nearby, and sat and watched a variety of birds tussle for the bounty. The bigger and stronger birds always got more, I noted in reflective mood, as with everything in life.

Near the greenhouse I have a small rose garden where I grow just one variety of rose for more dramatic effect – a hybrid tea called 'Ingrid Bergman', with a beautiful blood-red colour and tight centre. There was a droplet of water on an outer petal which acted as a prism when the sun caught it, and I gazed at it for some time, admiring its beauty while all sorts of thoughts raced through my head. I mused that I might have liked to be a gardener, one of the few things I'm good at (though when I once told Wilf that I had green fingers, he thought I meant I'd been painting my shed without gardening gloves on. He's a silly bugger at times). I was enjoying the moment when my mother reappeared with some news that was going to alter the course of my day – and indeed of the following months.

'Someone from the office on the phone for you, Steve.' Once again she gave me the benefit of her advice. 'You ought to get some new gardening trousers, they're in a right state.' She was right: they were torn and filthy, showing the ravages of time, but those trousers had been with me a long while, and we suited each other. Every time they were washed they came back with another tear, and as both Jennifer and Mother refused to mend them, I had taken to sewing patches onto the frayed parts, until I looked like the proverbial Joseph in his coat of many colours. I said it was a fashion statement, and Mother said I was a scruffy ageing hippy.

'Oh bother,' I said, or words to that effect, and answered the phone not with the usual 'Hello' but with the words, 'I'm not turning in today, Tracy. This is my day off, and you know only to ring me in an emergency.'

'Correct,' said Tracy. 'This is an emergency. We've got a murder. A bloke called Howard Fielding has topped his wife.' Tracy was becoming as blasé as me. 'You need to speak to DC Bull at

Rotherham police station – or do we give it to one of our competitors?' she asked dispassionately.

'I'll ring him, leave it with me,' I snapped. I'd known DC Norman Bull for some years. He'd been around the block a few times and had seen it all, but he was a good copper and a reasonable bloke.

While I waited for him to come to the phone, my mind conjured up all sorts of scenarios. Most murders are domestic, and I thought this was just another of those. Maybe a man who'd caught his wife playing away, or thought he had, or perhaps she'd complained a little too vociferously and he'd belted her with dire results – it was so easy for a simple argument to escalate into a murder scene. I didn't like human nature; I'd seen it at its worst. I was thinking that it must be wonderful to live on a hill in the middle of nowhere – no traffic, no policemen, no magistrates or judges, no staff, no Inland Revenue, no VAT man, no clients – when Norman came to the phone.

'Aye up, Steve, how's things? I think you might want to come out on this,' he said.

'I don't. I'm in the middle of an important duty.'

'Oh, you're in the garden, are you?' said Norman. 'What are you planting?'

'Tomatoes,' I replied.

'Are you using Money Maker?' – a very popular variety with Northern gardeners.

'That's the one,' I said. 'I've grown them from seed, and if I may say so, they're in fantastic condition...' We discussed Money Maker tomatoes for a minute or so. 'I may even put in ten,' I concluded.

'Bloody hell, that's a big greenhouse,' Norman replied. 'You'll be planting out now? Tough shit. As I said, I think you want to come in on this one. It's a tragic case and it's upset all the lads. Wait till you see this bloke, we feel so sorry for him.'

That intrigued me, because people in his job don't often feel sorry for defendants, and when an old hand like Norman Bull tells me a case is tragic, I believe him. 'What's gone off?' I asked.

'We'll give you full disclosure when you come, but the outline is that Howard's wife got Alzheimer's. They took her into hospital against his wishes, and decided that she should stay there, but let him take her home for the weekend – when he tried to poison them both to end it. He didn't pass away, but she did. He's in hospital, because they had to stomach-pump him, but they're releasing him this evening. Are you going to come down?'

'What time, Norman?' I asked, hooked. Whilst I really didn't want my day off interrupted, this sounded like a special case.

'About six. You should have got your tomatoes in by then. By the way, he's admitted it: he left a note saying he intended to take her life. Murder looks nailed on.'

I gardened until five, then showered and put my trusty trousers away for another day. A mile out of Rotherham I got stuck in a traffic jam opposite a tattoo shop: those days were the start of the strange culture of people decorating their bodies with weird and wonderful designs, and body piercing was also becoming popular, with people sticking stainless-steel bolts through their tongues, eyebrows and lips, and occasionally other places an ordinary person might think uncomfortable. I imagined myself walking into court with a bolt through my tongue and eyebrow – or better, one through each side of the neck, so I could pretend to be Boris Karloff. It would be funny in cross-examination, when the witness realised he or she was to be questioned by Frankenstein's monster...

The traffic cleared, I left the fetishist behind, and soon arrived at the police station, where I was greeted at reception by a new girl with a classic hotel receptionist twang: 'Good evening, my name's Gloria, can I help you?' I felt like asking her if she was impressed by people who had bolts through their eyebrows, but, noting a bolt through one of her own, decided against it and simply asked her to tell the custody suite that Steve Smith had arrived.

It was only a minute before Norman Bull arrived and took me down to the custody area, where we waited to catch the attention of the custody sergeant, a delicately pretty woman nicknamed 'Hard as Nails', since her looks belied her nature. She looked at me with her intense blue eyes and paused before she said smoothly, 'Good evening, Mr Smith.'

'Good evening, Sergeant, and may I say what a pleasure it is to see you again?'

'You can cut the crap, thank you, it doesn't impress me. Your defendant's called Howard, a very nice man we're all worried about.'

This was a remarkable comment from her; obviously Howard had made quite an impression. (I later found out that Hard as Nails had offered him her toast because, understandably, he'd not eaten for two days. *Nobody* gets her toast, so he was obviously special.)

I went into a small anteroom with DC Bull and a detective sergeant called Weir I hadn't met before, who was also sympathetic. He related the tragic events.

'About five years ago, Mrs Fielding started to become forgetful and prone to losing things. After about a year, it was so bad her family insisted she see a doctor, who diagnosed the early stages of Alzheimer's disease. You can imagine what the family felt about that. Well, after another two years the poor woman had completely lost it, and started to become violent – she would panic and hurt herself. Howard was the only person who could deal with her. Her daughters and son couldn't, even the people at the respite care centre couldn't, so it was all left to him.

'The kids had been trying to get her into a home for at least eighteen months,' he continued, 'because poor old Howard hardly ever slept. He dedicated his life to Joan, caring for her every need, but eventually gave in to the pressure to take her into hospital to be assessed. He didn't realise they would keep her in, and didn't like it. Nor did she. Though she didn't know who Howard was, she seemed to be aware that he represented some form of security, so when he left her at the hospital, in different surroundings and with different people, she was like a child, grabbing at his legs so he couldn't leave.

'When he went back to see her the next day, he found her sitting on the floor, half dressed, with food smeared over her face, and the lower half of her body covered in her own waste. For a man who'd cared for Joan every waking hour, it must have been a dreadful sight. He complained, of course, but in fairness her behaviour had been so difficult that the staff couldn't deal with her.

'It was the same story the next day, and this time he persuaded the doctors to let him take his wife home for the weekend. When he got her there, he bathed her, washed and dried her hair and manicured her nails, then gave her some food with a number of sleeping tablets crushed into it. He took the same concoction himself, then put her on the settee and sat by her side, waiting to die. He left a note stating his intention to kill, which makes it murder.

'Howard would have got his way, too, if one of his daughters hadn't called round to check all was well. She had a key and let herself in, which woke him up before he lapsed into unconsciousness. The drugs made him vomit, but he explained it away by saying he'd caught a virus, and his daughter went off reassured, without trying to disturb her mother. Howard took some more pills, thinking they'd be enough to finish the job, then in his confusion rang us to say what he'd done. But as luck would have it – if you call it luck – it didn't work.'

Sergeant Weir continued: 'When the police arrived, they found Mrs Fielding on the settee covered by a blanket, and the officers could tell at once that she was dead. Mr Fielding was sitting by her, half-conscious, holding her hand and mumbling to her. The ambulance arrived almost simultaneously with the scene-of-crime officers. Mrs Fielding was declared dead at the scene, and Howard was taken into A&E, where he was stomach-pumped. It seems clear from their report that he was traumatised; they kept him on twenty-four-hour suicide watch.

'The murder scene was remarkable because it was immaculate. The deceased was clean and tidy, with her hair recently washed and styled. All the dishes had been cleaned; there were no empty tablet cases or anything like that. Upstairs all the deceased's clothing was clean, ironed, and neatly put away; the washing basket was empty, and the wardrobe, drawers and bathroom cabinet were spick and span. On the kitchen table, the household documents, including insurance policies and the deeds for the house, had been laid out in order. Placed on top of them was a note, which we believe was written by Howard. It read—'

He produced a plastic bag, labelled 'Exhibit 1', which contained a note hand-written in block capitals by a man whose hand had been trembling slightly. Sergeant Weir cleared his throat, and read slowly:

'TO MY WONDERFUL CHILDREN,

FORGIVE ME, BUT I HAVE HAD TO TAKE YOUR MOTHER TO A BETTER PLACE. I CANNOT SEE HER END HER DAYS FRIGHTENED AND MISERABLE. SEEING HER IN THE HOSPITAL IN THAT STATE WAS TOO MUCH TO BEAR. I'M NOT GOING TO LET HER SUFFER ANY MORE, AND I CAN'T LET HER GO ALONE, SO I'M GOING WITH HER. IT IS FOR THE BEST. I HOPE YOU WILL FIND IT IN YOUR HEARTS TO FORGIVE ME. EVERYTHING YOU NEED TO SORT THINGS OUT IS HERE. GOD BLESS YOU ALL.'

Sergeant Weir stared at the document for some seconds, then handed it to me. No one spoke for what seemed an age. I read the words to myself, and when I looked up the two officers couldn't meet my gaze, almost as if they were apologising for what they had to do.

Eventually, I broke the silence. 'This isn't going to be an easy interview,' I ventured.

'No,' said Sergeant Weir, then tried for a silver lining to this particular cloud. 'But you'll like Mr Fielding. He's a real gentleman.' In all my years as a criminal lawyer, I had never found the police so much in sympathy with a defendant.

'I know you said on the phone he's physically fit for interview, Norman, but is he fit mentally?' I asked.

'Yes, we've cleared it with the hospital,' Norman said, not too happily.

'Okay. Just one other thing: how come Howard didn't die?'

'Well, we believe he ingested about the same amount as he fed his wife, but he's bigger and heavier. Then of course his daughter woke him in time to stop him from falling into a coma, and he vomited enough of it out of his system that the top-up he took wasn't enough to do the job before his phone call brought our boys there.'

'Do you accept that Howard intended to kill himself?' I asked.

'Unreservedly,' said Sergeant Weir firmly. 'Is there anything else, or do you want to go through?'

'Yes, let's go, please,' I replied.

I read through my notes as I waited for the prisoner to be brought into the interview room, thinking how paradoxical it was to interview someone about such a serious case in such a very small room. These interviews are probably the most important part of the prosecution case, yet the facilities available for them are poor.

As I pondered on this, the door opened and Howard walked in

He was of average height and weighed over twelve stone, with iron-grey hair pushed back rather unevenly, as though the task was only half-finished, and dark bags of exhaustion under his eyes. He was clean-shaven, and wore a pair of smart grey flannel trousers and a blue open-necked shirt – I could still see the creases down the arms where it had been ironed – but oddly, his feet were in slippers. His eyes, which darted around the room nervously before meeting my gaze, were red and clouded, and his face grey and heavily lined. He had the mark of death about him, a look I had seen many times before. But when we shook hands, his had a firmness that somehow gave me confidence.

I asked him to sit opposite me at the wooden table (which was bolted to the floor, as was the seat; the police don't like to have anything in interview rooms that can be picked up and used as a weapon). Howard eased himself into the seat with obvious discomfort, sighed, and stared at me expectantly, his hands shaking uncontrollably.

My first reaction was to ask him how he was feeling, a stupid question, but he replied politely, 'I suppose as well as can be expected.' We looked at each other as if we wanted to avoid the inevitability of what was to follow.

'I'm here to represent you, Howard, to look after your interests as best I can. I know this is going to be difficult, but the sooner we start, the sooner we finish. And first, so I can look after you properly, I need to trouble you to go through what happened.'

Even I could hear the reluctance in my voice, but Howard seemed resigned. 'I understand,' he said, trying to put me at my ease. 'You've got your job to do, as these other gentleman have, and I'll do my best to help you.' Then, without prompting, he began his story.

'I meant to kill her, you know. I planned it, I did it, and now she's gone. I knew exactly what I was doing, as I've already told the police, and will tell them again in the official interview. It doesn't matter to me now. My only disappointment is that the hospital saved me.' Tears welled up in his eyes as he spoke, and when he stopped he put his head in his hands and wept.

I appreciated why the police had told me about the suicide watch at the hospital. Here was a case with motive and planning – the clearest admission of murder one could ever hear, with no expectation of or desire for the perpetrator's own survival – and perhaps it would have been kinder to let him die. But this wasn't murder, despite all the boxes ticked in its favour. If we could just prove that Howard was suffering from such abnormality of mind at the time that he couldn't realise the nature of his act, we might be able to establish a case of diminished responsibility – which, roughly speaking, would make him guilty of manslaughter, not murder. In terms of sentence, the difference would be immense.

The moment was broken by DS Weir knocking on the door and bringing in two cups of tea. 'I thought you'd like a drink,' he said. 'Is everything all right?' he asked Howard. 'If you need anything, just give us a shout.'

'Thank you very much,' he replied. 'You've been so kind already.' But his hands trembled as he held the polystyrene cup, so some of the hot tea spilled onto his fingers. His face registered no reaction as he stared into the cup, his mind clearly beginning to wander, then he suddenly snapped back. 'I'm sorry, Mr Smith, I'd gone there for a minute.'

I smiled reassuringly. 'That's all right, Howard. Take as much time as you want.'

'No, I don't want to detain you. I don't suppose you've had your tea yet, have you?'

'Don't worry about me, Howard, I'm used to it – and so's my wife, luckily! Now do you mind if I ask a few personal questions, just to complete all these forms I have to fill in? First off – I'm sorry, but I have to ask – you're not going to do anything silly, are you? I mean, try to do anything to yourself?'

'Don't worry,' said Howard. 'My children made me promise. I've seen what this has done to them, and I'm not going to put them through it again.' And I believed him.

To break into the facts as gently as I could, I asked him to give me a potted history of his life. He told me he and Joan had met at thirteen, married at eighteen, and been together for sixty years since. They had three children, two girls and a boy. Howard had worked in the steelworks in Sheffield all his working life. He talked of their dreams of the places they would visit in his retirement.

The first fifty-five years were idyllic, then one day Joan put two sugars into Howard's tea, which he thought odd, because he hadn't taken sugar for over thirty years. He mentioned it and, as she clearly hadn't realised what she'd done, put it down to a lapse in concentration. But over the next few weeks he noticed further odd incidents. 'Age does play tricks with your memory,' said Howard. 'I didn't think it was any more than that, because we all forget things, don't we?'

He went on to catalogue a series of events that painted an unpleasant picture. For the first time in her life, Joan started losing her temper. The children noticed and persuaded him to take Joan to the doctor, but hugely offended by the idea that she might be losing her marbles, she refused to co-operate. About six months later, she found herself putting salt into a mixing bowl instead of baking powder. When Howard pointed this out, she was distraught. Howard finally made an appointment with the family doctor and explained what had been happening, and the Alzheimer's diagnosis resulted.

Listening to Howard, I could understand his suffering. With murderers who plan to kill their victims for practical reasons (usually their own survival), the interviews are much easier. But although Howard had elected to kill his wife, he had done so for what he thought was her own good.

In my line of work, you have to take sides. You're in your client's corner, so you do the best you can for him or her. And the law is a business too, so you have to think about your career and future. In that respect, I'd have represented Jack the Ripper.

Howard finished his tea and wiped his eyes with a handkerchief – pristine, neatly folded and ironed. I tried to lighten the subject by asking him who did his ironing.

'Well, me, of course,' he said. 'There's no one else to. It doesn't take long to become an expert.'

'How long have you being doing it, Howard?' I asked.

'Oh, about five years or so. I have to, for my wife…' His voice faltered as once again the realisation came home to him. 'Sorry, Mr Smith,' he mumbled.

'You don't have to apologise to me, Howard. I should be apologising to you, making you go through all this again. And please call me Steve,' I said, 'or you'll make me feel old.'

'I've been very lucky, you know, really,' he mused. 'I had a wonderful wife and children. I always had a job, and while we didn't have a lot of money, we never really wanted for anything. I always managed to get time off, and we had some marvellous holidays…' He paused, and I could see him reminisce, but I had to jog him back to the present.

'Can I ask you what happened when you went to the hospital, Howard?'

'Yes, of course,' he said. 'The doctor said Joan had to be assessed, but I told him I could cope – and I could, you know, I really could. But the children thought it would be best, so reluctantly I agreed, and we took her in. I knew she wouldn't like it – I could sense it when we were walking through the door. Joan sort of braced herself, and I knew what that meant.

'They were very nice to us, but it was a strange place to her, and although she didn't understand much by then, she could sense familiar people and surroundings. When you take someone in that condition out of that environment into something else, it's hard…'

His voice tailed off as he began to lose his composure again, but after a second or two he took a deep breath and went on.

'We were there for what seemed an age, and the doctor asked her all sorts of questions she couldn't answer – she was really too far gone – but when I tried to point that out they got shirty with me. I tried to tell them that she was a lovely lady, despite what she'd become. I told them she was beautiful, and I'd been the envy of all the steelworks because I'd married the best-looking girl in the area; all the blokes used to rib me about it. And I never once went with another woman, or even contemplated it... Anyway, the doctor told me he wanted to keep her in for assessment. I told him straight that they wouldn't be able to cope with her, they didn't understand her moods, but they wouldn't have it. My daughter told me they might even section her and take her in by force if I didn't agree. What do you do when doctors tell you what they believe is for the best?' He held up his hands in despair and continued.

'When I tried to leave, it was horrible. Joan got agitated, ran to me, almost as if she knew what was going on. I tried to calm her, but she was having none of it. They literally had to pull her away. My daughters took me out, but I could hear her cries. It haunted me all night; I couldn't sleep for worrying whether they would look after her properly.

'I visited the hospital the next morning to make sure she was okay and bring her fresh clothes, her favourite dress. But when I got there, you wouldn't believe what I saw.' Howard put his head in his hands as if to hide from some awful sight. After a time, he continued.

'There was food all round her face and even in her hair... She can't eat properly, you have to coax her, be patient and hold the spoon. They told me she'd just been messy when feeding herself, but she can't do that. They lied to me, and that upset me. But her personal state – if I can put it that way – was worse.'

Once again I found myself apologising for seeming to torture him with my probing, as Howard tearfully explained his wife's state.

'I took her into the ladies' to wash her, and the nurse came in and shouted at me for being there. I didn't know what to say. I know I shouldn't have been in the ladies' toilet, but pointing out the state Joan was in didn't seem to make any difference. I was sent away, and the same thing happened the next day. Thank God it was a Friday night, and they'd said they were very short-staffed at the weekend, so I persuaded them to let her come home with me for two days. But I had to convince *them* that I was capable of looking after her, when I'd gone back twice and seen her in that bloody state! Get permission from them to look after my own wife! I didn't dare say too much, because they were in control, but when they tried to contradict me I'm sorry to say I lost my temper and gave them both barrels.'

'Good for you, Howard!' I said.

'She'd never been in that state with me. I always put nappies on her, because she didn't know when she was...' His voice trailed off, leaving that part to my imagination. 'When I'd been with her about ten minutes she calmed down, and they could see the difference I'd made. But before I left, they told me Joan was going to have to stay there long-term. I couldn't bear the thought of going every day and seeing that. In just two days, she'd deteriorated so much... She'd been used to good and loving care, the way it should be. It was my duty, and she'd have done the same for me.'

He banged the desk, shocking both of us. It was time to take a break – we had been there for over an hour – so I came out of the cramped interview room and asked the sergeant if it was possible to have a cup of tea. It was enthusiastically supplied, and I returned to the room.

'I'm so sorry to put you through all this again, Howard,' I apologised again, but he stopped me in my tracks.

'It's all right, Steve, I know it's got to be done.'

Over the next thirty minutes, Howard explained how he had devoted the last five years of his life to the care of his wife, and said how lucky it was that Joan, who had been a proud woman, hadn't been aware of how cruel the disease had been to her.

'In the car Joan was agitated and thrashed her arms about, but I managed to calm her, and when I got her home I put her straight into the bath. Then I washed and arranged her hair, dressed her in her best frock and took her downstairs. I was talking to her all the time, you know – I always do that; somehow the sound of a familiar voice keeps her calm. I was telling her I wouldn't let them put her through that again, and that was when I decided to end it all – not just for her, but for me too, so she wouldn't have to go on her own. I told her what I was going to do, and it was almost as if she understood. I said to her, "We'll go together," and do you know, for one incredible moment I thought I heard her say: "Yes." But my mind must have been playing tricks on me, because she'd lost the ability to speak a long time ago.

'I crushed her sleeping tablets into a bowl of porridge – one of her favourites – which we ate together. I wasn't upset, I didn't feel regret, just relief – she'd suffered enough. I laid her down on the settee and covered her with an eiderdown to keep her warm, then got all my papers ready so there wouldn't be a mess for the kids to sort out. I left a note to try to explain what I'd done and why, then sat with Joan and held her hand while she fell asleep.'

'Can you remember anything after that?' I asked.

'Not really. I vaguely recollect one of the girls being there, and of speaking to somebody on the phone, but it's all very confused.'

'The police say you rang them.'

'Then I must have. They wouldn't lie.'

I asked Howard if he had known what he was doing at the material time: as this was a clear-cut murder, the only way for him to avoid conviction was to accept manslaughter on the basis of diminished responsibility. But he insisted, 'I knew what I was doing. I had every intention of putting an end to her existence – and mine – but unfortunately it didn't work as far as I was concerned.'

'Okay,' I said. 'I wonder if you fully understood my point, because I don't think I put it very well...'

'You put it very well, Steve, thank you. But I intended to take her life – and mine...' Once again his voice tailed off.

In the silence, all I could think of was Howard being found guilty of murder and sent to prison for life, the only sentence they could give him in the circumstances. At seventy-five, in his state of mind and health, he'd be dead within a year. I had taken on an awesome responsibility.

After we'd finished, it was time for the police interview. I was very impressed at how they conducted it: they were extremely gentle and more than fair. Throughout, they tried to get Howard to say he was very confused at the time, but he was adamant he had known what he was doing – which wasn't surprising, given how angry he was with himself for not having completed his plan.

In view of Howard's obstinacy, the interview ended sooner than I'd expected, and the police left us alone for a few moments.

'I'm going to apply for bail tomorrow, Howard,' I told him firmly.

'It doesn't matter to me, Steve,' he said. 'Do as you will.'

'But it's not just about you, Howard,' I said. 'What about your kids and grandchildren? You've got to think about them. They've already suffered one trauma – don't let them lose you as well.'

That seemed to strike a chord. 'I think the world of my kids and grandkids,' he said.

'Yes, so spare them a thought. You wanted to sacrifice all for your wife, so why not make a sacrifice for them by staying around, hard as that will be for you?'

Howard considered that, then asked, 'How are they?'

'Terrified that something's going to happen to you as well,' I said, lying through my teeth.

'All right,' he said eventually, 'I'll support you as best I can. You're a good man, Steve. Thank you for everything.'

I didn't feel like a good man. I had lied to a grieving man because I thought I knew best, but only time would tell.

As we emerged into the custody area, Hard as Nails asked considerately, 'Would you like another cup of tea, Howard?'

'Thank you very much,' replied Howard. 'I would appreciate it, when it's convenient for you.' It was odd to hear a defendant with manners, and interesting how the police responded to it: I think we all learnt a lot that day.

Sergeant Weir beckoned me back into the interview room. 'You know there's no alternative but to charge him with murder, don't you?' he announced as soon as the door was shut. 'But if he was suffering from diminished responsibility it'd be manslaughter, and he'd avoid a life stretch. I'm going to speak to the Crown Prosecution Service and tell them our opinion,' he said defiantly. I nodded, and agreed I'd see him at court the following morning.

As a criminal lawyer, you worry a lot about injustice. When you represent somebody accused of committing a serious crime and they get their just desserts, you're professional enough not to let it affect you. But when someone gets a sentence you believe is wrong, or is convicted when you believe they're innocent, it's an awful burden. In many ways, I wished Howard had seen someone from another firm, but we were stuck with each other now.

I arrived at court early, and found the Fielding family and a crowd of reporters waiting. The clerk wanted to call Howard's case in first, to get all those people out of his court, and I understood his point. Fortunately I was ready, as I had been rehearsing my bail application over and over in my mind.

The prosecutor, a friend of mine called Jim Scott, told me he wasn't opposing bail, which was a relief. All we had to do now was convince the magistrates, who in a murder charge have the power to grant bail but, if they do, must announce that they don't believe the public to be at risk.

I was forthright in my address, in the hope that the magistrates would not feel I was hiding anything and be afraid to grant bail – often, courts lock people up so as not to be seen to make a mistake. But we had a strong bench, and the chair was the wife of a doctor, so she knew all about Alzheimer's disease, which wasn't as well understood in the eighties as it is now. Howard was bailed on condition he live with his eldest daughter Joan and her husband. We dodged the photographers, and Howard was taken home.

I, on the other hand, had to represent Monica Redfearn, who had been caught soliciting outside Woolworth's. She had picked on an unsuspecting passer-by and, when he spurned her drunken advances, yelled at him, calling him a poof, fell into the road and had to be helped to her feet. She treated her helper too to a volley of abuse, and was promptly arrested by a PC Parfitt, a spotty young bobby who looked at least seventeen, whom she also reduced to the rank of poofdom. Fined £75, Monica complained bitterly that it was because she was skint that she was reduced to prostitution, and the magistrate's decision would send her straight back to the streets. Fortunately, the magistrate overlooked being called a 'twat'.

Monica had been refused legal aid, but her kids were good clients of mine so I said I wouldn't charge her, and she offered to 'see me right', with the words: 'If you're ever up my end, look in!' I shuddered at the thought.

The next bright spark I had to represent was none other than Elvis Presley – or that's who he said he was. He didn't look much like Elvis Presley: he didn't have any sideburns, or indeed much hair at all, and it certainly wasn't black. The middle of his head was bald, with 'Oxo' tattooed across it; he was about five foot one tall, with a large beer belly and a personal odour problem.

I assumed he was a devotee of the music, but asked his reason for the name change anyway.

'It's better than Eric Clamp,' he replied.

'Yes, I can understand that,' I said.

He had been charged with stealing scrap metal, which I thought was a big come-down for such a great star as Elvis Presley – reduced from playing to fabulous theatres in Las Vegas for megabucks, to pinching copper piping from a scrap merchant's yard in Rotherham.

'What were you going to do with the metal?' I asked him.

'Weigh it in at a scrapyard,' he replied.

'Not the same scrapyard, I hope,' I said jokingly.

'No, because that's where I pinched it from,' he explained, entirely missing the irony.

We decided he should plead guilty, and in view of the fact that Elvis had done this before, it was probable the court would want to adjourn the case for a probation report on how to sentence the ageing rock star. We went into court, and the chairwoman of the magistrates looked at her list, as was her wont, identifying each defendant.

'Which of you is Elvis Presley?' she asked. No one answered, so she directed the question at me.

'Which one is Elvis Presley, Mr Smith?'

I couldn't resist it. 'Madam, he's the one with the blue suede shoes.' Everyone on the solicitors' bench and a few in the public gallery thought my comment amusing – but Elvis didn't get it, and interrupted to point out that he was wearing white trainers.

Having been identified, he pleaded guilty, and the case was adjourned, as I had predicted. Elvis was ordered to see the probation service and come back to court four weeks later. Leaving the courtroom, he was heckled by some yobs in the public gallery who had come in to get out of the rain with comments such as 'Sing us a song, Elvis' and 'Give me one for the money'.

Unfortunately Elvis failed to collect his bail form, and as a result the chair of the magistrates snapped at me, 'He's gone without his bail form, Mr Smith,' as though it was my fault.

'I'll ask the usher to catch him, madam,' I said, and did so. A few moments later the usher reappeared and said breathlessly – and totally unaware of his own wit: 'Madam, Mr Presley has left the building.'

I'm not sure if the bench ever understood why I collapsed in tears of laughter.

Some six weeks later, I received a psychiatric report on Howard Fielding. I turned to the final page to read the conclusion before anything else.

'...in my opinion, Howard was suffering from such abnormality of mind that he did not know the nature and quality of his act, and consequently was suffering from diminished responsibility at the time of causation.'

I breathed a heavy sigh. 'Thank God for that!'

It seemed that our consultant had liaised with the prosecution consultant, which is quite normal in the circumstances, and reading the report in full it became clear that they shared the same view. All we needed now was for the prosecution to agree a guilty plea to manslaughter on the basis of diminished responsibility and the judge to accept it. Then we'd worry about the sentence.

A copy of the report was sent to the probation service, who had to see Howard so they could compile a report for the judge. Not surprisingly, their report was excellent, and concluded that this killing had not been conducted out of malice. What should you do with a seventy-eight-year-old man of previous good character who is never likely to offend again? Yet a life had been taken.

Eventually the day of judgement came. The case had been placed in the list of the most senior judge in Sheffield, noted for being a hard sentencer. The grey, overcast weather as I set off for Sheffield Crown Court didn't make me feel any better. The chill in the air gave way to a cold breeze that made me shiver as I entered the austere stone building.

Howard and his family were sitting in the waiting area just inside the main door, his daughters on either side of him, holding his hands. They stood up when I walked in; we all shook hands, and Howard greeted me with a smile. What do you say to a man who is about to be sentenced for manslaughter? I settled for 'How are you?'

I took Howard upstairs to an interview room where our QC was waiting to see us – Jeremy Baker, an accomplished advocate who had dealt with manslaughter cases many times before, some of them with me. I felt that our preparation was the best we could have done, and that we were now in the lap of the gods, rather than that of Mr Justice Skelthwaite.

At exactly half past ten the usher called Howard into court, and as we walked inside, Howard turned to me and said: 'I'd just like to thank you, Steve, for all you've done for me and my family. We appreciate it. No matter the result, you've done your very best.'

'Thank you, Howard,' I replied. 'And for being the ideal client. I only hope it works out for you.'

He looked at me and smiled. 'I'm not bothered about me; it's them,' looking towards his children. He embraced them all, then walked into the dock, where the prison officer took him into a back room to perform the usual search. The only thing Howard had on his person was a photograph: I couldn't make out the subject, but I could imagine who it was.

There was a buzz of anticipation as Howard re-entered, then in walked the rotund yet distinguished figure of Mr Justice Skelthwaite. The court stood in silence as the clerk announced, 'Would all persons having anything to do before my Lords the Queen's Justices draw near and give your attendance.' All the lawyers bowed, and everyone sat, except Howard and the prison officer in the dock.

The clerk of the court identified Howard, checked his name and address and date of birth, and put two counts of the indictment to him. 'Howard Fielding, count one of this indictment, you are charged with murder.' He read out the charges, then asked Howard to plead. He looked at me nervously, and I mouthed the words 'Not guilty'.

'Not guilty,' Howard said unfalteringly.

The clerk spoke again. 'Howard Fielding, you are further charged on count two of the indictment with manslaughter.' Again he read out the details; again Howard looked at me nervously, and seized the front rail of the dock as if he would fall if he let go. I mouthed the word 'Guilty'. Howard licked his lips, and his voice broke as he said, 'Guilty.'

The prosecuting QC was a large man, whose bulk was squeezed into a suit at least one size too small; his wing collar was hidden by his heavy jowl. His face was red, and there were beads of sweat running down each temple – he was either under stress, or suffering the effects of too much Burgundy the night before. He coughed a smoker's cough and addressed the judge in a deeply resonant voice.

'Has Your Lordship had the opportunity to consider the psychiatric reports in this case?'

'Yes, I have,' Mr Justice Skelthwaite replied carefully.

'Well, My Lord, I now indicate to you that the prosecution would be content to accept a plea to manslaughter on the basis of diminished responsibility, unless of course Your Lordship has any observation to the contrary.'

The atmosphere could have been cut with a knife as the judge flicked through his papers in a theatrical show of scrutiny. He had clearly read the case papers and knew exactly what he was going to do. The problem was, he was the only person who did. It was almost as if he was enjoying tantalising the courtroom with his show of deliberation. Then he looked up.

'What say you, Mr Baker?'

Jeremy stood up, tugging at the top of his gown to ease it into its rightful place. 'My Lord, I respectfully concur.'

The judge nodded thoughtfully. 'Yes, I think that must be right. But now, Mr Baker, what do you say about sentence?'

Quietly, calmly and succinctly, Jeremy set out the painful background for the judge. After that work of art, the judge proceeded to pass sentence.

'Howard Fielding, you have pleaded guilty to manslaughter on the basis of diminished responsibility, and I have read the reports about you from two psychiatrists. The prosecution has seen fit to accept the plea on that basis, as do I.

'Taking of a life in any circumstances is a matter of profound seriousness.' At that point I was convinced Howard was going to be sent away, because of the inflection in the judge's voice. He went on to point out that if people were allowed to take the law and circumstances and the choice of life or death into their own hands, we would have a very 'dangerous world'.

'We know that,' I muttered under my breath. 'Get on with it!'

'It is difficult to imagine a more painful sight for you on that fateful day in the hospital. I am satisfied that you are an honourable man, who did what you did with the full intention of taking your own life to put your wife – and indeed yourself – out of what you perceived to be complete misery.

'I also have to take into account the welfare of the public, and I am satisfied that you are not a danger to anyone except perhaps yourself. I do not, therefore, conclude that the public are at risk from you, and I cannot see that the public interest will be best served by sending you to prison.'

I took a sharp intake of breath.

'For those reasons, I shall take what many people may think an unduly lenient view, and I'm sure there will be many who will criticise me for it. But I do not think it appropriate to impose any penalty other than a conditional discharge for two years. This means that if you commit no offence punishable with imprisonment within the next two years, you will hear nothing more of this matter, but if you do commit an offence you can be dealt with for this case as well as the new one. In view of your age and personal circumstances, I do not impose any financial orders. You are excused.'

There was an outburst of cheers and clapping from a relieved public gallery. I breathed a sigh of relief, and Jeremy Baker turned, handed me his endorsed brief and smiled. I turned to look at Howard, expecting to see his face full of joy – but he wore the same resigned expression. He had clearly meant it when he said the outcome didn't matter to him.

He was reunited with his family outside, and they all thanked and congratulated Jeremy, then, one by one, came to shake my hand. Howard was the last to do so, and he said, 'You're a good man, Steve, a good man.'

'And so are you, Howard. It's all over now,' I said confidently.

'No,' said Howard, 'it's just the beginning.'

I thought for a moment and realised that he was right.

As I walked back to my car, I turned to watch Howard and his family walk the opposite way, into the distance. Just then the sun broke through, and Sheffield didn't look as grey as it had when I turned up at court that morning. On the drive back, I could see hedgerows bursting into leaf, and marvelled at the wonder of nature and what beautiful things there were all around us. My thoughts returned once again to Howard and his wife. I'd never been in favour of euthanasia before, but I am now.

ELEVEN

KEITH GLEESON'S COCK

Early one afternoon I came back from court to find Tracy presiding over a waiting room peopled by a galaxy of characters reminiscent of the Rogues Gallery at Madame Tussaud's. She pounced on me. 'Can I have a word, Mr Smith?'

'Of course, Tracy.' As she led me to the back room I smiled placatingly at the waiting clients, implying that I wouldn't keep them long; some smiled back, some grunted, and one was fast asleep and couldn't care less. One young woman at the end of the queue had a cut eye and a lump the size of an orange on her cheek, partially hidden by a bloodstained handkerchief. On automatic pilot, I asked, 'Are you all right?' Stupid question.

Tracy shut the door firmly behind us, and gave me her report. 'We've got one drunk who's not sure where he is, but I'm sure it shouldn't be here, and you've seen the lady with her face bashed in by her husband. He's sitting in their car opposite, waiting for her to come out so he can do the other side,' she said. 'We also have two conveyancing clients, but I've had to put them in the back tea-room, because they weren't impressed with our visiting drunk. Mr and Mrs Haigh have just married, and the drunk asked Mr Haigh if he'd come with his mother.'

She was interrupted by the sound of someone vomiting. I gazed at the ceiling for inspiration, then went out to reception and surveyed the damage. The drunk had at least tried to leave the room in time, but hadn't made it. A quarter of his dinner and the remnants of about eight pints of lager decorated the floor near the outer door, and he was trying to stagger back to his seat.

I barred his way. 'You're not coming back in here after that,' I said firmly, ushering him outside.

'Now then, Mr Burtoft,' said the drunk, 'You can't treat me like that.'

'Mr Burtoft may not be able to, but I can,' I replied. 'His office is next door. Good day.'

The man slid to the floor. In view of the witnesses, I resisted the urge to kick him down the steps, but propped him in the doorway of the office next door, where I left him sleeping soundly.

We were cleaning up when a representative of a local religious cult came in looking for donations. He was bald, apart from a strand of hair which curled down his shoulder in a small plait, was wearing what appeared to be a loose-fitting dress in bright orange, and had bells attached to his fingers.

'Have you got anything I can take?' he asked diffidently.

I looked down at the pile of vomit, and back at him, and he smiled as if he knew what I was thinking. 'Have I called at an inopportune time?' he continued – just as an aggressive figure appeared in the doorway, bringing a squeal of fear from the lady with the damaged eye, who ran into the back room. The figure entered and shouted gruffly, 'I want my wife! Bring 'er out 'ere or I'll fetch 'er!'

He pushed his way past the holy man, and I had a decision to make. Did I bar his way and risk being assaulted, let him go and do goodness knows what to his wife, or do the chivalrous but possibly foolhardy thing and hit him with the office hammer, which conveniently was stored in reception? I was reaching for the hammer when the holy man sprang forward, grabbed the man by the neck, and in one swift movement pushed his arm up behind his back. With an eerie calm he said, 'Peace, brother. We don't want to cause anyone any suffering, do we?'

The infiltrator yelled in pain, and bellowed. 'Get off me, you bald-headed bastard, before I smash your face in!'

'I don't think you're in a position to do that, brother,' said the holy man. 'We can either talk about this sensibly, or you'll have to wait here until the police come. It's up to you. Stand still now, or I'll have to secure my grasp by increasing the tension upon your arm, and your shoulder will be dislocated. I can assure you the pain will be intolerable.'

After a few seconds the aggressor realised that he had lost. Tracy phoned the police, and within a very short time the holy man delivered the bully into the waiting arms of two burly officers, who took him away yelling: 'I'll get you for this!'

The entire reception gave the holy man a round of applause, and I asked in astonished admiration, 'Where did you learn that tactic?'

'The Paras,' said the man. 'I used to be in the army until I found the light. Would you like a leaflet?'

Too grateful to refuse, I took a leaflet and pushed a five-pound note into his collection box. 'Bless you, brother,' said the holy man, waved his arms around demonstratively and rang the little bells on his fingers before marching out. I turned to the rest of the people in reception, and said, 'Well, I think we need a cup of tea all round. Please give your orders to the receptionist, and I'll be with you shortly.'

I walked into the back, and found Marilyn Hitchin cowering in one of the interview rooms. 'It's all right now. The police have got him,' I reassured her.

'Thank God,' she said. 'He's made my life a misery since he lost his job. He seems to think it's my fault.'

'Well, the nearest one always gets the stick,' I suggested. 'Look, I think the best thing we can do is to see about getting you an injunction. Have you got anywhere else to live?'

'Yes, I can go back to my parents. But they're elderly, and I don't want him there causing trouble.'

'I'll start proceedings for an injunction straight away, and we'll get you into court tomorrow morning. I suppose he caused your injury?' I asked sympathetically. She hung her head in shame and nodded, looking relieved as I set about completing the paperwork. I noted that, despite her injuries and dishevelled condition, she was an attractive woman of about forty. But when she gave me her birth date, I learned I was ten years out.

'So you're thirty?' I asked.

'Yes, that's right,' she said, 'although I feel a lot older.' I didn't comment.

'I think I'll have to go for a divorce,' she said. 'I can't put up with this any longer.'

'Well, in my experience, if it happens as frequently as it's happening to you, it won't get any better. You have to decide sooner or later whether you're prepared to put up with it,' I announced firmly. She nodded reluctantly, and her hands shook as I passed her a biro to sign the legal aid forms. Fortunately there were no children to be used as pawns in the game called 'matrimonial proceedings'. No one wins in those circumstances. I explained to her what to expect at court, and arranged for one of the secretaries to drive her to the hospital for treatment. A quick phone call to her parents ensured her transport home, plus a sympathetic ear to listen to the events of the day.

My next client, Jackie Hampton, was angry at having injunction papers issued against him by his estranged wife, who alleged that she had been subjected to matrimonial violence.

'She's a complete git,' said Jackie. 'She exaggerated everything in that affidavit. It makes me out to be a right bastard.'

I took the affidavit and read out a catalogue of sinful allegations, which certainly bore out that assessment.

'You know me, Steve, I don't knock the wife about,' he continued righteously. 'All right, the odd slap when she's deserved it, but that's normal, innit?'

I didn't answer, but reached for my notebook to list Jackie's observations on the allegations, which were supported by evidence that made the case against him look impossible to defend. When I told him so, he announced that he would represent himself, which would sort everyone out, and left complaining bitterly that the law was one-sided in favour of the woman. 'Peace, brother,' I thought as he slammed the door.

My last client interview finished, I trod the weary path up to my own office to go through the day's post. Land Rover had written to say that their vehicle was the best 4x4 on sale, but a letter from a Japanese firm disagreed with them. A Lincoln man wanted sponsorship to enable him to climb Mount Kilimanjaro in a polar bear outfit to raise money for the disadvantaged in Peru. Somehow I couldn't quite see the connections between Tanzania, polar bears and Peru – not to mention Lincoln.

The letters from clients in prison were always the best, and it was interesting to see how quickly new inmates acquired the prison 'twang'. Certain catchphrases spread like fleas in the confined quarters: 'Hey man, I need some warmth in the lungs' meant 'Hello, old chap, may I have one of your cigarettes, please?' and 'Hey, Captain, my head is in bits' meant 'Being locked up is having a profound effect upon me.' Sometimes I was promoted, as in 'Hey, Colonel, these four walls are doing my head in,' which roughly translated as 'As my respected solicitor, you should realise that I am finding it difficult to function in a custodial setting without access to women, cigarettes, drink and drugs.' It was a source of amazement to me just how many defendants laid claim to neurological problems, with such sayings as 'It's in my 'ead, man' and 'My 'ead can't accept it, man.'

That day I had one letter from a regular called Eric Wilkes, who had a growling, gravel voice thanks to his sixty-a-day habit. Since the one pound ninety-six pence a week he received for sewing mail bags provided only twenty roll-ups a day, and thin ones at that, an intolerable state of affairs which could not be allowed to continue, Eric saw it as my duty to provide him with a postal order each week so that he could increase his consumption to a more acceptable level. In addition, he had little or no entertainment during the day, and thought that this could be alleviated by my sending him a radio and supply of batteries. I dictated an answer regretting my inability to send Mr Wilkes his tobacco and a ghetto-blaster, since my finances were 'in bits' and my bank manager was 'doing my head in, man'.

It was an odd profession, I thought. You laboured intensively at your studies to achieve high qualifications, and bore the responsibility for a client's liberty, only to be treated like a cross between an errand boy and a general retailer. For the first time in my career, it dawned on me that I was not as happy as I had once thought. But I always believed in the Micawberish attitude, and the following day I was proved right.

The Honourable Sean Page had visited the Cross Keys in search of some meat and potato pie, good company and ten pints of Stones bitter – he never liked to overdo it at lunchtime. Uncharacteristically he was carrying a plastic shopping bag, which appeared to have a quill of some sort sticking out of the top, and with my usual curiosity I asked what treasures were hidden inside.

'Oh, it's a brace of pheasant, old bean. Old Wagger caught one up the arse with the side by side, so the old girl's going to shove them in the oven and we'll have pheasant for dinner.' Pagey always adopted this 'British Raj' idiom. He puffed on a large Cuban cigar as he expounded the virtues of pheasants, saying authoritatively, 'They've got to be well hung, don't you know.'

'Haven't we all!' replied Wilford, as he started his fifth pint.

Pagey thought this hilarious, but as his booming laughter subsided, my peripheral vision spotted a familiar face entering the pub. Dealing with criminal work, you soon learn the knack of three-hundred-and-sixty-degree vision, enabling you to spot bandits and scroungers from all angles. A Mr Bumble-like figure, resplendent in blue shorts and a Manchester United football shirt with short sleeves, which exposed a variety of artistic tattoos on powerful arms, with a dark Che Guevara moustache, receding hair, glasses and a lisp, approached me almost secretively. It was a client of mine called Keith Gleeson, a likeable man, and from his manner I inferred he had weighty matters to impart.

''As tha got a minute?' asked Keith surreptitiously. 'In private like...'

We left Wilf and Pagey and went to sit at a small table out of earshot of any other customers. I put my pint on the table and gazed at a clearly worried Keith Gleeson, who absently downed my pint before launching into his problem. 'That bastard Trevor's had my cock!' he exclaimed.

'I beg your pardon?' I asked, taken aback.

'Yes,' said Gleeson, 'A beautiful cock an' all, one of the best-looking parrots you've ever seen... the bastard!'

Keith was a forthright man but you did sometimes have to guess what he was getting at. 'Wait a minute, Keith,' I said. 'Let me see if I've got this right. You have a cock-bird parrot that Trevor has stolen – is that what you're saying?'

'Not really,' said Keith, ''E owns the cock. But it's the 'en, she needs 'im!'

The picture was becoming no clearer. 'Just what has gone off? What's the crack?' I asked, using a well-known Rotherham expression.

'Tha sees, I've a 'en bird, Esmeralda, and it was just old enough to be mated, so Trevor came round to my 'ouse one day and told me. 'E knows a bit about cocks, an' 'e said that, because 'is one and Esmeralda were the same family of bird, we should breed with them. I know enough about it to know that, if it had three or four eggs and they 'atched, when the birds are grown up a bit they'd fetch about five 'undred quid each.'

'Really, as much as that?' I asked.

'Oh aye,' said Keith, 'There's big money in parrots. Anyroad, you're supposed to leave the cock with the 'en after it's laid an egg and when the young'un's born, otherwise the 'en bird will fret. Well, what happened, she 'ad three eggs, that meant one apiece.'

'That's two,' I interjected.

'Aye, and one for grabs,' he continued. 'Trevor an' me couldn't agree on 'ow to do it – there were no point me giving him 'alf an egg, were there? – so we fell out. Then one day 'e came down to the aviary and just took the bloody cock away. When I got up next morning the 'en had pulled all its feathers out.'

'Why had it done that?' I asked, sympathetic but mystified.

''Cos it were in a fret, and when they fret they pull their feathers out. It looks a reet mess.'

'And what about its mental state?' I asked.

'Oh, it just sits in its cage and shivers, like,' said Gleeson. 'Tha'd feel cold if tha were a parrot and somebody pulled all thy feathers out. Anyroad, I'm not going to interrupt tha chat with tha friends,' he continued, having already done so. 'I can bring Esmeralda round to see thee, if tha likes.'

'All right, Keith,' I said. 'I've got some time free about five o'clock this afternoon. Bring her in then and we'll see what we can do.'

'Reet,' said Keith. 'I don't want to take the law into my own 'ands and give 'im a bit of four by two, but it's cruel. You shouldn't be cruel to defenceless animals.'

As we walked back to my friends, I repeated to Keith that I would look into the case, and he should bring Esmeralda into the office later that day. He turned to leave with the parting shot, 'So far as I'm concerned, with that bastard Trevor, it's t'cock or else!'

'What the bloody hell was that about?' said Wilf.

'Oh, he's got a bit of a problem with a bird.'

'Oh,' said Wilf, 'bit of two-timing, eh?'

'In a way,' I replied, not wishing to go into detail.

'What's Esmeralda look like, then?' asked Pagey, who had obviously caught the name. 'She sounds like a bit of a goer.'

'I think she's African,' I said, 'and she's pulled all her feathers out.'

Pagey looked at me quizzically. 'Wears a headdress, does she?' I didn't bother to elaborate. We were at cross purposes.

At the office I found a large bag of parrot seed on the reception desk. 'Mr Gleeson left it. He says he'll pick it up in the car later,' said a confused Tracy.

'Well, don't eat all of it, then,' I replied as I collected my messages. 'Anything important happened, Tracy?'

'No,' she smiled. 'Do you want me to keep the birdseed here, or are you going to take it?'

'No, I'll let you look after it,' I said, returning her smile. I spent the next ten minutes on the phone to a friend from the county court. We concluded that Keith could issue a summons in the county court, but because the value was only small he could actually represent himself. Then I thanked him for his valuable assistance, and he thanked me for the best laugh he'd had that week. I wrote out a full list of instructions in the hope that Keith might be prepared to represent himself, and turned to my mixed bag of afternoon appointments.

Midway through the afternoon I felt hunger pangs, and as my four o'clock appointment hadn't turned up, I nipped over to the off-licence across the way for a chocolate bar, plus a six-pack with which to entertain my guest later that afternoon. That would mean one can for me, two cans for Gleeson and three for Wilf, who would make his feelings clear if he didn't benefit from the transaction.

As I crossed back to the office, the sound of a van horn seized my attention, and a white Luton van pulled up abruptly. I recognised the driver as Craig Twates, a likeable lad employed by his mother Ursula in her light haulage business, which operated around the South Yorkshire area under the name of 'U. Twates'. Ursula was an honest but fearsome woman, and Craig, who was terrified of her, wanted my advice about a minor shunt he'd been involved in while making a delivery – he was 'bricking it', to use his expression, at the idea of confessing the damage to his mother.

I told him that the accident would have to be reported to his insurance company, and apparently Ursula dealt with all company correspondence, so he was left with no alternative but to tell her. In this job you sometimes have to give people news they won't like, although some clients think that you can wave a magic wand to solve their problems at a stroke. He drove off rather dispiritedly in the direction of the family premises, and as he pulled out, I noticed the company name – U. Twates – affixed by sticky letters on the side of the van, had been doctored: somebody had mischievously removed the 'e' and the 's'. It was Rotherham's graffiti experts showing their usual sophisticated humour.

About five Mr Gleeson duly arrived, carrying a large cage which appeared to have been draped with someone's curtains. He put it on my desk and unveiled the object, announcing proudly, 'This is Esmeralda.'

I was shocked to see a sickly looking bird, completely bald apart from two or three tufts on the top of its head, and looking as though it had been primed for the oven. I couldn't think of anything to say except, 'Hello, Esmeralda.'

Esmeralda did not reply, but Keith spoke for her. 'She's not very happy.'

'I can see that,' I said thoughtfully. 'It was a white parrot, then?' I asked.

'It was,' said Gleeson dejectedly, 'but she's not now.'

I explained to Keith that there would be an argument concerning ownership, but if the court believed his version and we were able to prove that the bird was 'fretting', he was in with a chance of a court order being granted returning the cock bird for such time as was necessary. I added that as it was unlikely legal aid would be granted, if I prepared the court pleadings he could conduct the case himself. He wasn't impressed, so I changed the subject. 'Can it speak?' I asked inquisitively.

'Argh,' said Gleeson, 'but only one word. Knackers!'

'I beg your pardon?' I said in surprise.

'Knackers!' repeated Gleeson. 'Our lass taught 'er. It's 'er favourite word.'

It was time to bring the conversation back to the question of court proceedings.

'Does tha mean I'll 'ave to go to court on my own?' asked Gleeson despondently.

'Well, yes, but you can tell the story very well.'

'Argh, but what if 'e has a solicitor with 'im? It's going to be a bit one-sided then.'

'I don't think he will, Keith. You can't get legal aid, so nor can he.'

Gleeson lowered his chin and thought for a moment before announcing, 'I'll see thee reet. I don't expect thee to do it for nowt.'

The prospect of representing this unlikely bird fancier in the county court, with other solicitors taking the mickey, filled me with dread. County court has different rules and procedures from criminal court, and requires a quite distinct approach – not to mention a stiff collar, which I can never do up in a hurry, which I always am. Let's just say it wasn't my strong point, and all I needed was some smart-arsed judge who knew all about parrots asking me questions I couldn't answer, and my life would be turned from moderate happiness to complete misery. Nevertheless, I felt sorry for poor old Gleeson; the bird obviously meant a lot to him, and he was one of my most loyal clients. Once again I was faced with a case I didn't want, and a feeling in the pit of my stomach that all was not well.

After a quarter of an hour of bartering, Gleeson left, having promised me a free parrot from the next brood. I was reflecting on this when Wilf opened my door. 'Have you got any of that lager left?' he enquired.

There was one can left, the one reserved for me, and my eyes moved to the right, where it was standing. Wilf's did the same, and it was almost as if we were two gunfighters waiting to see who was quickest on the draw. Wilf won, and strode out majestically with the can.

'You don't want to share it, then?' I shouted.

'Sorry, I didn't hear you,' said Wilf.

'That's all right,' I said. 'You'll not have heard we've just bought an office parrot, either, will you?'

Wilf's door slammed firmly shut – I don't think he liked parrots – as Sheila appeared, ready to leave. 'Do you need me for anything else?' she asked.

'You don't know anything about parrots, do you?' I asked.

'Don't be daft,' she said. 'I'll lock up then.'

I wondered what the reception area would look like with a large parrot cage in the corner, whose occupant repeatedly shouted 'Knackers!' at my visitors. As I packed my things, I realised I could well have made a grave error of judgement.

TWELVE

GOOLE, GLORIOUS GOOLE

Although most of my work was in the immediate South Yorkshire area, I was asked to work in the 'foreign' courts from time to time. Whilst it's nice to get out of one's home town occasionally, it can be a nightmare if you have to visit two courts on the same day. It's always a dilemma which court to go to first, since it is vital that you get on first to avoid being late for the other court. Sometimes it works out beautifully, but more often it doesn't, and that's when you find out what stress is all about. The days are gone when courts were happy to adjourn for a cup of tea and mid-morning chat while they waited for your grand entrance: we all now have to deal with too many cases in too few courts, and magistrates get understandably irritated by delays. During my time in the legal profession matters have got steadily worse, and in the mid-eighties the best years were already over, certainly for legal aid practitioners.

Solicitors are often seen as consumer-unfriendly 'fat cats', and large firms with massive private practices do earn substantial sums – which they would say is consistent with the difficulty, responsibility and importance of the work they do. But the average legal aid practitioner does not aspire to such financial glory, let alone attain it. He has to work extremely hard, be prepared to turn out at any time of the night, deal with all sorts of obnoxious characters, submit to bullying by certain of the judiciary without the right to answer back, and then fight for his fees at the end of the day. A week shadowing your average legal aid practitioner would be an eye-opener, to say the least.

So it was that I found myself considering the list for the following day with cases in Rotherham, Sheffield and Barnsley, plus an important drug case in Goole. I could give the cases in Sheffield and Barnsley to an agent (another solicitor who would act as my stand-in) but the Goole case was likely to end up at the crown court, the two defendants were in custody and wanted to apply for bail, and one of them was a regular. Danny Newton had been charged with possessing heroin with intent to supply, alongside his girlfriend/common-law wife Davina Chester. At thirty Danny already had a number of convictions for drug-related offences, symptomatic of his need. A bright lad, he had done well at school, but at the age of seventeen opiates entered his life, bringing the side-effects of dishonesty and an ever-increasing irrationality.

So far that week everything had gone well, but experience told me the bubble would have to burst, and Goole seemed as good a place as any for it to happen. My journey took about forty-five minutes, and being early I found the court was closed, so decided to look for a bacon sandwich as the best way to start the day. I found a decent-looking coffee bar on the main street, where I ordered two bacon sandwiches and a hot chocolate before being directed to a table and told that my order would be delivered 'as soon as Edie gets back from the lav'.

As I studied the morning paper, three old ladies came in, ordered tea, and sat at the table opposite. I couldn't help but hear the conversation.

'Oh, she 'as suffered,' said the fat lady.

'She 'as that,' said the tall lady.

'They were just like grapes,' said the fat lady.

My sandwiches were delivered and I tucked, closing my eyes and sitting back in unconfined pleasure.

''Ave you seen them, then?' asked the small lady. 'I don't think I'd like to.'

'You'd get a shock,' said the fat lady. 'I've never seen anything like them, she couldn't walk a straight line.'

'They say tight belts and sitting on wet seats brings it on,' said the small lady.

'Get away,' said the tall lady. 'I've got a tight belt but I've never 'ad them.'

'It runs in the family, so they say,' said the small lady.

'Well, it galloped in 'ers,' said the fat lady seriously. 'Just like grapes, they are.'

I was just about to finish my first sandwich when the tall lady said, 'She wants to go and have that done.'

'I don't think she'll do that, there's far too much pain. They 'ave to sit on a tyre for a month, you know,' said the fat lady.

'Well, 'ow does she go on when she 'as to… you know?'

'Perish the thought,' said the fat lady. 'Are we paying a call?' They all agreed, and I finished my second bacon sandwich and fled before they reappeared.

It was 9.30 am, and the courthouse door was ajar, a cleaner busy sweeping the entrance. 'Can you tell me which way to go for the prisoners?' I asked politely.

'Next door, police station,' she said abruptly. 'They don't bring them round here till 9.45, the clerk's most specific about that. He doesn't like to be messed about, likes to get on with it; everything has its place and it's all got to be on time. There's some don't like him, but I don't care, I do my job and go. Anyway, try the police station. I've got to get on, I can't spend my time talking to you.'

I'd heard Goole was an unusual place, but hadn't realised just how many unusual people lived there. I made my way to the police station, where my two prisoners were brought into the interview room by a burly-looking policewoman with a deep voice, who locked the door behind her when she left – which seemed a touch unnecessary, as I couldn't imagine any would-be escaper getting past her.

Before I could greet them, Danny and Davina were locked in a seemingly endless embrace. 'Excuse me,' I said. 'Sorry to be nuisance, but do you think we could have a chat about these charges?'

They both giggled as they sat down at the table opposite me, but I was in no mood for levity. So I said in my best serious-lawyer fashion, 'I might as well tell you from the start, these charges are serious. You've both got possession of Class A heroin and possession with intent to supply. There's a third charge of supplying someone called Sean Caxton, whoever he is, and the case will certainly go to the crown court, because I gather they collected about a thousand pounds' worth of heroin from the house.'

'Not guilty,' said Danny. 'Have you got any fags?'

Davina made no reply until Danny nudged her, then she sighed, 'It's all down to me. I'm guilty and I'm admitting it.'

I had the gut feeling that all was not well.

When I went into court, the CPS representative was unloading three large black bags of files onto the bench in front of him, and looking extremely harassed.

'Good morning. I'm Steve Smith, solicitor from Rotherham.'

'Huh,' came the reply.

'I'm sorry to bother you, but I wonder if I might ask you about the case of Chester and Newton.'

'I haven't seen half of these files, which the police have just given to me, late, and I don't know how people can expect I should know anything about them. There's at least an hour's worth of reading material here. It's absolutely disgraceful.'

'I'm sorry about that. Would you like me to come back later?' I said, sympathetically.

'No, I suppose I'll have to deal with your query now,' he said impatiently. 'Which case was it?'

'Chester and Newton.'

'Never heard of them. Are you sure it's in the court? I've not seen that file.'

I looked down at the pile of files on his desk and spotted the Chester file under 'C'. 'This is it, I think,' I said.

The CPS man's embarrassment only increased his annoyance. 'What is it you want to know?'

'Only whether you're opposing bail.'

He fumbled through his papers. 'It's supply of drugs, according to this. Of course I'll be opposing bail.'

'But the girl has no previous convictions at all.'

'Well she will have after this. This court won't even try it, they'll send her to crown court.'

'But that's no reason for refusing bail.'

'It is here,' said the prosecutor. 'The court clerk, Mr Croft, has a downer on drug cases.'

'Well, it's not for the court clerk, is it? It's for the bench,' I said as pleasantly as I could.

'That's what you think... No, I'm applying for custody for both of them. I'm sorry, I've got to read the rest of my files now,' he said, and turned away.

I could understand his annoyance: the pressure was on him with only ten minutes before the bench came in, when he'd be bombarded with queries from all angles, and after all, I was a 'foreigner' from Rotherham.

We were joined by the court clerk, a tall, grey-haired, distinguished man of about sixty, who was even snappier than the prosecutor and viewed me with suspicion. I smiled and offered my hand, as I'd been taught, but Mr Croft was unimpressed and ignored both.

'I have the case of Chester and Newton. It's a bail application and the prosecutor is asking that the case goes to crown court.'

Mr Croft turned his back to me, putting some papers on the magistrates' bench behind him. I tried again.

'My name is Steve Smith, a solicitor from Rotherham. I'm here to bother you with the case of Chester and Newton, a bail application.'

'Yes, it will bother us. We've a horrendous list today.'

'Well if it helps, I've seen my clients, I know what the application is going to be, and I'm ready.' There were no other defence solicitors in the courtroom, so I thought this was my opportunity to get called on first.

'You're in the ten-thirty list,' said Mr Croft forcefully, 'It's five to ten now, and I can't call you until ten-thirty. You'll have to wait for the other cases.'

By this time my patience was fraying. 'What other cases?' I gave an exaggerated look around the courtroom. 'I don't see any other solicitors waiting.'

'Oh, there will be,' said the court clerk, and turned away.

I sat at the solicitors' bench and set out my papers in readiness. It was like *High Noon*, when the tension builds up as people watch the clock, and Mr Croft was standing anxiously hoping the solicitors from the ten o'clock list would come into court and push me to the back of the queue.

The magistrates walked in at one minute past ten and bowed graciously; the chairman, middle-aged with a pleasant face, looked a bit louche in his sports coat and a maroon shirt, especially as he was flanked by a lady of similar age in tweeds and pearls, and a gentleman smartly dressed in a conservative suit with white collar and tie. 'May we call the first case, Mr Croft?' said the chairman, smiling at me, clearly expecting that that would be mine, as I was the only solicitor present.

Mr Croft asked the usher if any of the solicitors for the ten o'clock list were ready, and she hurried out, to return three or four minutes later and say they were all busy in conference and not immediately available. 'Have we any unrepresented defendants in the ten o'clock list?' asked Mr Croft.

By this time I was becoming a mite agitated at the disgraceful way I was being treated. The fact that I was from out of town should have made the court call my case first out of courtesy: at

Rotherham, if we have a solicitor from a different area we always give him precedence if at all possible. But in Goole, it seemed, the tradition of politeness to solicitors from 'out of town' had been lost.

The usher told the court that the only unrepresented defendant had decided to see a solicitor after all, and was waiting for one to come free, and the chairman turned to me. 'Do you have a case?' he asked.

'I do, sir. My name is Steve Smith from Rotherham and I represent Chester and Newton,' I said, then couldn't resist adding, 'but I am told they are in the ten-thirty list.'

The court clerk turned to the bench and confirmed, 'Yes, they are in the ten-thirty list. I wonder if Your Worships would like to retire until one of the other solicitors is ready?'

I tutted furiously, and addressed the bench. 'Sir, with great respect to your learned clerk, I am sitting here waiting, I have a case ready, and although it's not in your ten o'clock list, rather than retire and do nothing, would Your Worships kindly consider dealing with it?'

The chairman spoke briefly to his two colleagues before announcing, 'I don't see why not, Mr Smith. Could you call on that case, Mr Croft?'

Mr Croft threw his pen to the desk, shot me a venomous glance, and with great reluctance took my papers out of the ten-thirty pile of documents in front of him. The CPS man leaned across and whispered, 'You'll not get bail now.'

The defendants were brought in, and while Mr Croft read out the charges I studied them carefully. On the one hand there was Danny, who was beginning to show the tell-tale signs of addiction – a discoloration under his eyes, a constant sniff and excessive sweating, and an inability to remain still. Then Davina, standing with her head bowed in shame, a pretty girl who looked far younger than her years, since the drugs had only just begun to rob her of her youth and, although not gifted with great intelligence, generous of spirit and gentle by nature. Her parents were honourable, hard-working people, he a bus driver and she an assistant with the school meals service, who had built a decent home in a reasonable suburb of Rotherham where their daughters were well provided with education, home comforts and love. But they had become estranged from Davina over her dependence on drugs and on Danny, with whom she was besotted; her younger sister, who adored her, hadn't seen her for over a year. Such family tragedies were an inevitable side-effect of drug-taking.

'Did you say this is an application for bail?' asked Mr Croft.

'Yes, Your Worships, for both defendants.'

Mr Croft tutted. 'I'm afraid it's a full bail application, Your Worships, despite our list,' he clarified unnecessarily. I resisted the temptation to empty the contents of my fountain pen into his ear, and studied my notes.

The prosecutor opened with the facts, which were that for three days the Drug Squad had kept observation outside the house where Davina and Danny lived – but whose tenancy was in Davina's name only, a point on which he made great play. During that time no fewer that thirty people visited the house, five of whom were stopped and searched afterwards, and all found to be carrying small quantities of heroin, which they all stated they had bought from someone in the house, although none of them named anyone. The next day the police had raided the house and found a thousand pounds in cash, a hundred individual wraps of heroin with a street value of about the same amount each, a set of chemist's scales and a lot of small plastic bags. The frequent visitors and drug paraphernalia indicated that Chester and Newton were both mainstream suppliers, and accordingly they were both arrested. Whilst both defendants had denied the charges during interview, the evidence was sufficient to justify them.

Mr Croft nodded knowingly, as though the decision had already been made. I made a bail application, pinning my hopes for Danny on the fact that he was not the tenant of the house, so although he was resident there at the time of the transactions, he wasn't necessarily involved in them. For Davina, I pleaded that she was of good character and unlikely to reoffend if given help for her drug problem. But the drugs obviously belonged to somebody, and it had to be one of them, which rather limited the force of my argument.

The bench retired, and were out for some time. After a while, the bell rang, summoning Mr Croft to advise them. 'That's the end of that, then,' said the CPS man, and sure enough, within minutes the clerk returned with the bench, and announced remand in custody for both defendants. I went to the cells afterwards to point out that they could make a further bail application the next week, but I wasn't too hopeful. Danny was annoyed, but Davina said nothing.

The next week I got to Goole a little late, owing to circumstances beyond my control, arriving at ten past ten. I went to see Davina and Danny in an interview room, where they were sitting holding hands. Danny was pale and looked ill, but Davina looked quite well after the week's remand. 'I'm pleading guilty,' she said. 'It's my responsibility. Danny didn't know anything about it, and it's my house anyway, so he wasn't in a position to stop me.' She looked at Danny for acknowledgement; he smiled, squeezed her hand and looked back at me.

'I'm not guilty, Steve. You heard what Davina said. We want to make a bail application for me and she stays where she is. I've got to look after the house, and a million other things, so I've got to get bail. Davina's all right. She'll get some bird, but she'll have a better chance at getting weighed off if she's had some time on remand.'

'Very convenient,' I thought. 'Why on earth is this girl letting this happen?'

'He's right, Mr Smith,' said Davina. 'It's got to be this way.' It was pointless to discuss it further, so I went into the court at twenty-five past ten, to be greeted with a nod from the CPS man, in a much better frame of mind than the week before.

It was after ten-thirty when Mr Croft and the bench reappeared from their deliberations, and the defendant in the dock was duly despatched to the Fine Office. At this point, Mr Croft saw me. 'I'm afraid you were in the ten o'clock list,' he said smugly. 'Since it's now after ten-thirty, other cases have to take precedence. If you'd been here on time you would have been called.'

I rose to my feet and addressed the bench. 'Your Worships, I'm sorry I wasn't here at ten o'clock, but there were difficulties on the M18. I then had to go to the police cells, where my instructions were of such importance that I couldn't deal with them in just five minutes.'

'We appreciate that,' said the chairman helpfully.

'I'm sorry, sir,' interjected Mr Croft, 'but we must now concentrate on the ten-thirty list.' And the chairman nodded, as if he'd been admonished by an overbearing headmaster, and another case was called on.

Despite my fury, I couldn't help being interested in a middle-aged man who had pleaded guilty to six charges of indecent exposure, or 'flashing', and asked for eighty other offences to be taken into consideration – and apparently had had three previous appearances before the court in five years for the same offence. The chairman of the magistrates decided that he wasn't going to be 'let off' this time, and imposed a substantial fine, but the wording of his sentence provided a great deal of amusement for everyone in court. His sermon of reproach went something like this:

'You've done this on three previous occasions, when you were bound over and conditionally discharged but here you are, before the court again for the same thing. This time, we are determined to make you feel it through your pocket.'

Many of the solicitors could not contain themselves and had to leave the courtroom smothering snorts of laughter, but Mr Croft totally missed the point.

When the eleven-thirty list had been dealt with, there was no one else left, but even then my case was called on at ten past twelve with great ill will. 'And if it isn't finished by one o'clock, you'll have to come back at half past two,' announced Mr Croft evilly.

'Of course, but I hope we can manage it before then,' I said politely, resisting one of my more primitive urges. I made the bail application for Danny, because both my clients insisted on it, but with the greatest reluctance. It was true that Danny had denied the offence, it wasn't his house and there was no evidence that he had actually sold any of the drugs, so the case against him was weak. The bench retired, and Mr Croft was not called for.

They returned just before one o'clock, so I would be able to get to Rotherham for the afternoon court. Davina was remanded in custody, having made no application, and remarkably Danny was bailed, subject to fairly restrictive conditions.

I went to see Davina in the cells afterwards. 'It's all right, Mr Smith,' she assured me. 'I'm going to use the time to come off the drugs. Danny's going to get us a house in another area, and when I'm released we'll settle down. He says we can get married while I'm in prison.'

I smiled, but made no reply, and returned to Rotherham wondering what Davina's parents would think of their eldest daughter becoming a jailbird. Struck by melancholy, I wondered if mine was such a good job after all. Had I wasted all the years of training, reading and learning? Did I serve a useful purpose, help the administration of justice? My answer to each question was negative. For the past few months I had dealt with nothing but junkies, judges and jail, and I was sick and tired of all three.

While Danny was released scot-free, Davina's case was adjourned for four weeks for probation reports. I was convinced she had taken the rap for Danny, but she would have none of it. Besides, she argued, if he'd been convicted he would have got six years because of his record, whereas she would get less as she had no record, so they would be apart for a shorter period if she admitted the offences.

She was right in that. The judge sentenced her to three years, as a deterrent to other drug-dealers, since in the court's view she was just another junkie asking to be put away. I asked her if Danny appreciated what she'd done, but she maintained that their relationship would rise above the sentence and the opinions of an 'out of touch' judge. 'Well,' I said finally, admitting defeat, 'I hope he's worth it.'

'He is,' she said defiantly. I nodded, and maybe she thought that meant I agreed.

Some nine months later, I was passing Clive's Jewellers in Rotherham when I saw Danny Newton walk out with a girl who, from the back, looked exactly like Davina. Then I realised she couldn't possibly have completed her sentence, unless she'd got parole, so I decided to catch them up to see what was going on.

The pair stopped outside the café next door, where they were joined by another young lady, who examined a ring on Danny's escort's finger. As I drew level, I heard her say, 'Congratulations to you both.'

Fortuitously, a group of people came out of the café just then, hiding me from Danny's view. The girl wasn't Davina, but someone very similar – and heavily pregnant. Danny now has three children by this lady, although they've since separated and he lives with someone else. I haven't seen Davina since that day at Goole, and neither, I understand, have her family.

THIRTEEN

ANYONE FOR CRICKET, AND SPIDER'S REUNION

June is supposed to be a month of good weather, and in 1987 it actually was. I was looking forward to a Saturday with the lads at the Abbeydale Cricket Ground, Sheffield, to watch Yorkshire play a county match. Jarvis had got tickets for me and my partner Steve Wilford (who was more interested in the bar than the bat and ball). Our builder friend Bodger Broom was taking the day off from a contract he had at Jarvis's to join us, together with Tenbelly Norman, gourmet and beer-drinker supreme, Lewis Frame, the mad Scotsman, Timbo Johnson from the Bradford and Bingley Building Society, Mike Walker, manager of Whitegates estate agents, and bringing up the rear none other than the Havana cigar-smoking Sean Page. In a sensible moment I'd thought of asking for our managing clerk Roy to be included, to keep us in some sort of order, but with me and Wilf both out, someone had to mind the shop. Besides, with Pagey involved, it was a futile hope anyway.

Jarvis had arranged for a minibus to take everyone to the ground and bring us back in the early evening, but I had to make my own way, because inevitably I had the morning court. Though I enjoyed weekends out with my pals or pottering in the garden with my family, workaholism born of insecurity kept me wedded to Rotherham Magistrates' Court. However, I hoped to finish my list by about noon and be at the ground for lunch.

My last client of the day, Trevor Wardle, had been up to his old tricks of fiddling one-armed bandits and breaking into cars, but he claimed he'd turned over a new leaf and decided to join the army. To prove his point he produced a copy of an application form to a local regiment, which included a list of questions of the variety: 'Have you or any of your immediate family suffered from any of the following, and if so, state the relationship of the sufferer.' Good old Trevor had ticked 'congenital heart disease' and specified 'step-father'.

I tried to point out this inaccuracy. 'But Trev, your stepfather's congenital heart disease is irrelevant. They want details of your family history.'

Trevor thought for a minute, then asked blankly, 'What's irrelevant mean?'

'That it doesn't matter,' I clarified. 'Your stepfather isn't a blood relative, which is what counts. You see, if your father was bald and your grandfather was bald, it's a safe bet that you'll follow your family history and go bald too.'

Trevor thought again. 'Me father wasn't bald, he still ain't, so I'm aw reet there, ain't I? Me stepfather is, though.'

This was going to be difficult. I asked, 'Do you know anything about genetics?'

'Aye,' said Trevor triumphantly. 'Great group, love their music.'

'Yes, all right,' I interjected, 'but as far as this form is concerned, family means the same bloodline. So your stepfather isn't a relative in this context, OK?'

'Why not?' asked Trevor.

I gave up and returned to his charges. He reluctantly agreed to guilty pleas to all four of them, and the magistrates adjourned the case for probation reports before they sentenced him. As I was being given the date for the adjourned hearing, Trevor tapped me on the shoulder and said urgently, 'Don't forget to tell them about the army.'

'I will,' I assured him – but sadly, four weeks later he was given a three-month sentence, thus missing his interview with the regiment.

Now I could go to the cricket! But as I left the courtroom, the emphysemic usher told me that a prisoner, brought into the cells on warrant because he'd failed to attend court on the due date, had asked for me. I sighed, and turned down the spiral staircase to the cell area, where I could hear the jailer on the phone, talking about 'some twat'. I hoped he didn't mean me.

Eventually, he appeared at the gates and asked who I wanted to see.

'I don't know the name – a new prisoner who's been arrested on warrant.'

'Aye, more paperwork to fill in. Why can't the bastards turn up on time?' he chuntered as he opened the door. Still looking forward to the cricket, I tried to cheer him up.

'Not to worry, we'll soon be out of here and home, Derek.'

'Like bleeding hell you will. Got another bastard coming in in half an hour. Been on the run; he ought to be shot with shit. I'd drown the buggers, or shove a red-hot poker up their jackseys.'

He opened the door to Cell 1, the executive suite with the broken toilet, and out came a dishevelled, sickly looking youth called David Selby, who had what looked like burn marks down one side of his face and on his hand. The hair on one side of his head was also frazzled, so it didn't take Sherlock Holmes to work out that he had been involved in some sort of fire.

In the interview room, Selby sat down opposite me with a sneer on his face, and threw his charge sheets on the table. He had been charged with the attempted theft of copper cable, the dream of every would-be tatter (a man who collects scrap metal), because of its high scrap value, but he unfolded a fantastic story to account for it. Apparently, while walking his dog on an embankment on the way to Sheffield, the dog ran after a rabbit. In his haste to retrieve the dog, Selby slipped down the bank, and reached out to grasp something to break his fall. Unknown to him, the something was a metal saw, which then came into contact with the copper cable and caused an explosion.

'An explosion?' I asked incredulously.

'Aye,' said Selby. 'T'cable was live, carrying power from one pylon to another. I was blown into t'air and burnt me face, arm and body. I came to in t'hospital, and they said it were a miracle I worren't killed. Me 'air's been curly that side ivver since.'

'You mean to say that you grabbed a saw by accident, and by another accident the saw ran across some copper cable and electrocuted you?' I always try to temper my enthusiasm for my job with self-control and courtesy, so I chose my words carefully. 'That's the biggest load of bollocks I've ever heard,' I announced.

'Tha doesn't believe me, does tha?' asked Selby disappointedly.

'Correct,' I said. 'And nor will the court.'

Selby looked hurt, so I said sympathetically, 'I'm only trying to help you, David.'

'Well, believe me, then,' he said sarcastically. A high percentage of criminals won't face up to the inevitable, wriggling and arguing that black is white, but the court usually imposes a stiffer sentence if it feels it's been messed about.

'David,' I persisted, 'if you plead not guilty, you'll lose the case and probably your liberty as well.'

'Tha means bird?' he asked, using one of the slang words for prison. 'Fook me!'

'Yes. I won't mislead you.'

Selby hung his head and sulked. 'I'm not guilty, and I'll get off with it. I'll get a solicitor who'll fight, not give in.'

'Well, I wish you the best of luck.'

'I don't need it, I'm not guilty. Thanks for nowt.'

I gave him his papers, and he left in search of another solicitor who would do his bidding – and I finally then set off for the cricket.

It was twenty past two by the time I got there. Lunch had been cleared away and the only drink left was medium white wine, which I hate, so I settled for a glass of iced mineral water and went off in search of my friends. Given that Wilf and Pagey were involved, the bar was the obvious place to look, and sure enough, there was the gang, listening to Tim's latest joke while another reprobate, Julian Binney, went round collecting for the kitty.

Bodger announced that he had a cert at Haydock Park called Method Actor, having been told by a former jockey that it couldn't fail.

'Why is he a former jockey?' I asked.

'Suspended for illegal betting,' said Bodger.

'Oh, marvellous! I suppose he's the most reliable source, then,' I said. 'What are the odds?'

'Eight to one now,' said Bodger. 'But I dunnow what they'll be in an hour.'

'Let's have a go,' shouted Pagey. 'Fiver each.' Everyone agreed, and Wilf turned to me. 'Lend us a fiver.'

'Bloody hell, Wilf, you took twenty-five quid out of the petty cash this morning!'

'Yes, but I had to get the first round.'

Begrudgingly, I handed over a £5 note for him along with my own, and Pagey volunteered to go to the bookies. It was 3pm and not one of us had seen a ball bowled, so the rest of us decided to go out and enjoy an hour's cricket before tea.

It was idyllic. The sun was shining, the air dry and warm, and the gentle breeze carried the smell of freshly mown grass. I was sitting with my pals with a pint of Guinness in one hand and the remnants of a pork pie in the other, amidst fields which were a stunning mixture of greens, from bright emerald to a soft bronze. 'At its best, this country takes some beating,' I announced proudly.

'It certainly does,' said an Indian gentleman wearing a turban sitting next to me, with whom I then enjoyed a long conversation about the beauty of our respective countries until a large cloud scudded across the sun, blocking it from view. Further clouds appeared, and in minutes it was quite dark. Just as I was about to warn the group of the prospect of rain, it started, and the stand emptied.

We watched the television in the bar as Method Actor romped home by three lengths and we all had £50 each to come – or would have, if Pagey had backed it. But he had apparently decided Pile Driver was a better bet, and had put all our money on him.

Following his confession, there was a chase round the ground as Pagey tried to escape the clutches of a number of highly emotional punters.

Michael Wellington McIvor, otherwise known as Spider, was one of my most loyal clients, with a face ravaged by a tattoo artist's needle. His forehead bore the words 'Ford Cortina Mark IV', the favourite motor vehicle of the local villains, but the tattoo which dominated his face was of a large spider in an even larger web, extending from his cheekbone to his neck, and about his chin small spiders completed the family portrait.

Despite that, Spider was an inoffensive lad, abandoned by his alcoholic mother – who had no idea who his father was – when Spider's child benefit stopped. He had lived in a variety of children's homes until he was eighteen, but remarkably he wasn't bitter, and always spoke fondly of his mother. Unfortunately, his desire to be noticed led to the disastrous tattoos, which drew attention to him in the wrong way. The jeering taunts of his peers and his resultant loneliness made him easy meat for unscrupulous rogues who used his longing for friendship to their best advantage – and that was the direct route into drugs.

Drugs featured more and more in the criminal courts in the eighties, only the names changing as a new word entered the criminal dictionary. The 'junkie' had been born, and was living in

Rotherham as well as just about everywhere else in the United Kingdom. The sequence from junkies to judges to jail was quickly established, and I was seeing a lot of all three.

Spider had already served two prison terms, which only deepened his own addiction, wantonly fostered by those who used him as a small-time pusher and delivery boy, so I was resigned when he turned up in my office with a handful of crumpled charge sheets alleging that he had possessed and intended to supply cannabis, heroin and ecstasy. There was no allegation of supplying drugs to anyone specific, the evidence of intention to supply being inferred from the quantities found in Spider's possession – in other words, there was far too much for one person to use, so the likelihood was that he was selling it to others.

I completed a legal aid application, then asked what plea he was going to enter. 'Guilty,' said Spider firmly.

'We've had this conversation before,' I replied. 'You don't expect me to believe that you managed to lay your hands on approximately five thousand pounds' worth of dope on your own, do you? Spider, you've only just done two years for drug matters. You were covering up for someone else then, and you're doing the same now.'

'Whose side are you on?' shouted Spider.

'Your bloody side!' I shouted back in frustration. 'Can't you see I'm trying to help you? You'll go down for at least five years this time, and where will your druggy friends be then?'

'I did it, and it was mine,' insisted Spider doggedly.

'Then find someone else to represent you. If you think I'm going to let you take the rap this time, you're a bloody idiot!'

Even before I saw the hurt in his eyes, I regretted saying it. Everyone had called him an idiot all his life, and now I, his solicitor and confidant who should know better, had done the same. Spider bowed his head, avoiding eye contact, and slowly reached out for the charge sheets, then rose and walked out, still with his head bowed. 'Shit!' was the only word that came to mind.

A fortnight later I was in the magistrates' court when the usher, through coughs, called out the names of defendants who were to grace Court Number 1 with their presence, including one Michael Wellington McIver.

There was a ripple of laughter along the court corridor as Spider came into view, represented by one of my competitors. He kept his head down in an attempt to conceal his face, and listened intently as the prosecutor read out the facts of the case – which the magistrates declined to deal with, on the grounds that their powers were insufficient. It was adjourned for eight weeks, during which the CPS would prepare the case papers before serving them for Spider's final appearance at the magistrates' court and committal to the Sheffield Crown Court itself. From there, I suspected, he would be rapidly dispatched to Leeds Prison by a grumpy crown court judge who disliked junkies, solicitors, and the human race in general.

Later that day, at the police station, I ran into Detective Inspector Desmond Lightowler of the Drugs Squad, who was new to the area, wanted to be a superintendent by next week, and believed that convictions led to promotion. He was one of a new breed of policemen, a high-flyer aiming to achieve the highest rank possible – and everyone who knew him thought he would do it, unless his enemies got to him first. Tall, plain of face but bright of eye, with tightly cropped black hair and a swarthy complexion that would require two shaves a day, he was a snappy dresser who always wore a suit, shirt with a starched collar, highly polished shoes, and his tie in a Windsor knot. It was rumoured that his marriage was foundering on the reef of his relentless ambition: he was certainly one of the hardest and most uncompromising men I've ever met.

'It's over for McIver,' he said knowingly. 'We've got him game, set and match.'

I saw no point in arguing with him. Clearly the police had

simply accepted Spider's admissions and closed their file. They were wrong; he was no more than a messenger boy. But in taking the blame for someone else he had lost most of his mitigation, and the court could only sentence him on the basis that he was indeed a mainstream supplier.

Next Wednesday evening, my football team played the Probation Service, during the day a group of caring, tolerant gentlemen, who worked hard to reintegrate criminals into society. But on the football field they changed – I sustained more injuries against the Probation Service than any other team, as they relieved the frustrations of their day. Since solicitors had a similar duality, the pitch often became a battlefield.

Owing to absenteeism, we had drafted in Bader Lister's brothers Barry and Peter. Barry was a skilful player who always seemed to have plenty of time to make the ball do just what he wanted, and Peter's turn of speed on the wing would leave you gasping. Peter was on majestic form, and by half-time we were 3–0 up.

During the tactical team talk we all drank copious quantities of Lucozade while our goalkeeper, Big Norm, drank two cans of Guinness. He wasn't a particularly good goalkeeper, but the fact that he weighed eighteen stone gave him the ability to narrow the angles, using his huge frame to get in the way of the ball. He was one of those players who either had a good game or a very bad one, but in this particular match his positional play was inspired, even if he did annoy everyone by sipping from a can of Guinness during the match itself.

The game ended 4–2 in our favour, and any annoyances disappeared over a couple of pints of beer in the bar, where the Probation Service enjoyed our hospitality, particularly the pork and dripping sandwiches we had named 'Cholesterolville'. Everyone went home happy, but in the morning I woke up in agony from the excesses of the night before.

As I limped up to the court, I ran into Big Brenda Dobkin and her Rottweiler/Alsatian cross Tiger, who wagged his tail furiously during our conversation.

''E's a good boy,' approved Brenda in her deep, resonant voice, 'but 'e 'ates postmen. Every time 'e sees one in his postie uniform, 'e goes mad and tries to gerrim.'

The dog licked my hand affectionately, leaving it full of slobber, then shook his giant head, coating my trousers with more.

'See 'ow he likes thee? But you watch 'im wi' a postie's uniform, 'e goes berserk. I reckon one must have kicked 'im when 'e was young. They don't forget, you know.'

'No, of course. Anyway, I'll see you again, okay, Brenda?' I said, and limped up the court steps. The corridor was full of the usual suspects, a veritable rogues' gallery representing the seamier side of the Rotherham criminal classes. The defendants there for simple motoring offences stood out like sore thumbs, resplendent in their best suits, sporting attaché cases, clutching their summonses, hand-written sheets of mitigation and letters of support from their area managers. The rest of the clientele wore jeans, T-shirts and trainers that had seen better days, and clutched other people's attaché cases they'd nicked earlier on.

I shouted the names of my clients, greeting those who answered and then discussing how we would proceed with their cases. The three courts sitting that morning were all occupied with other cases, which gave me time to visit the WRVS canteen – and there sat Terry Jordan Fitzgerald, reading a pornographic magazine with the word 'nudist' in the title. Terry's name sounded as though he should be an author, but the only thing he had ever written was a forged sick-note for one of his court appearances. Over six feet tall and about nineteen stone, with a shock of carrot-coloured hair, a dreadfully spotty complexion which had never seen a hint of Clearasil in his twenty-four years, and buck teeth, Terry was a small-time crook specialising in thefts from motor vehicles;

what he didn't know about tyres and wheel-trims wasn't worth knowing. Despite his failings, Terry was likeable, an unintentional comedian who made people laugh by accident – especially at his stutter, which affected certain letters more than others and particularly the letter 'F', often leading you to think he was about to swear.

Feeling expansive for some reason, I decided to treat him. 'Cup of tea, Mr Fitzgerald?' I offered. He didn't hear me, his attention fixed firmly on the centrefold of his magazine. I acquired two polystyrene cups of a dark brown liquid posing as tea, and sat beside him. 'I've no whisky on me, so it's straight tea, Terry,' I said.

'F-f-f-fine by me,' said Terry, then returned to his studies. I looked over his shoulder at a picture of numerous naked men and women of all ages, shapes and sizes in a variety of unusual poses, attempting to look as though they were acting normally. 'I didn't know you were into naturalism,' I said.

'F-f-f-f-found it on the bench,' Terry grinned, and continued to read.

'What you in for, then, Terry?'

'F-f-f-f-found a tax disc, and coppers say I nicked it. It ain't nicked, and I'm going to tell 'em. Will it take long?'

'Probably,' I said. 'Especially if you represent yourself. But do your best.'

Terry looked up briefly from his studies, and began, 'F-f-f-f...' I was out of the door and on my way to Court 2 before he got beyond that.

I finished that case, and was fighting my way through the smoke and grime of the court corridor when Spider appeared. 'Can I have a word, Mr Smith?' he asked.

'Yes, of course, Spider,' I said, and took him into the rat-hole.

'I just want to say sorry I see'd another solicitor.'

'That's all right, Spider, no offence taken,' I lied.

'Well,' said Spider, 'I want to change back to you again. This bloke treats me like a knob-head.'

Of course, Spider was a knob-head, but I was overtaken by sympathy, and also secretly pleased by his loyalty, something alien to many of the characters we had to represent.

'And I've got some good news for you,' he continued. 'I've signed myself in for a detox, starting tomorrow. I'm sick and tired of drugs. I don't think it'll take long, because I've not been out long enough to get back into it in a big way. My probation officer's fixed for me to go into t'ospital, and I'm going to give it a go.'

'Well done, Spider!' I replied enthusiastically.

'There's another thing,' said Spider seriously. 'Do you think if I get these tattoos off my face, people will stop laughing at me?'

I couldn't help admiring his intentions. 'Yes,' I replied confidently, 'I think they will.' That finished our conversation, and Spider set off for the clinic.

A fortnight later, purely out of interest, I rang his probation officer to see how he was getting on. He had completed his detoxification programme, and his last urine sample had confirmed there were no drugs in his system. He had also kept an appointment with a plastic surgeon ready to sort out his tattoos.

Over the next four weeks, while Spider waited for his case to come up, he tested negative for drugs at each check, a date for the first operation on his face had been fixed, and the icing on the cake was that the Probation Service had traced his mother, and was trying to reunite them. On the day he reappeared at the magistrates' court for committal to the crown court, Spider was happier than he'd ever been. All this built up considerable mitigation – which probably wouldn't save him from a prison sentence, but might well shorten it – and the magistrates gave him a date for the crown court some eight weeks hence, which would allow him time both to have the operation and meet his mother.

Then, one Monday, Spider phoned to give me a new address: the drug barons for whom he'd worked had discovered his whereabouts, and paid him a visit to say they were none too happy at his retirement. He had resisted their advances at the cost of a black eye and broken nose, declined to make a complaint to the police, but had had the foresight to see his probation officer, who got him rehoused. I praised his resolve to free himself from the drug scene, and hoped against hope. The harsh reality was that the drug barons had far more resources than the forces of law and order.

Spider also asked if he could meet his mother at our office, since his new bedsit was in a shared house that offered no privacy, and he didn't want to meet her at social services' premises, the venue for their meetings before their separation. I therefore set aside one of our conference rooms for the meeting, installed a coffee machine, and got Sheila to rustle up some sandwiches and a couple of cakes.

I returned from court at 1pm to find Spider sitting in reception, dressed in a new suit, a white shirt and a tie clearly selected for him by someone with dress sense. His hair had been cut and styled, and his face and hands were spotlessly clean, but unfortunately these improvements only accentuated the dreadful tattoos. He was sitting nervously on the edge of his seat as if waiting to be interviewed by the CID, but when I came in his face lit up.

'You look very smart, Spider,' I said admiringly. 'In fact if that suit was a bit bigger, I'd borrow it off you. What time's she due, then?' I asked.

'Any time now, Mr Smith,' he replied. 'I haven't seen her for years, you know, so I don't suppose she'll recognise me. And of course there's the tattoos. I don't think she'll be impressed, but I've got a letter to show they're being taken off.'

'Very good,' I said, 'If you'll forgive me I've got to do some dictation, but feel free to wait here for her, and stay in the room for as long as you want.'

As I turned to leave, Spider called after me, 'Thanks very much, Mr Smith. I'll not forget you for this.'

'That's all right Spider, I'm happy to oblige. Anyway, you deserve it for the efforts you've made. How's life?'

'Oh, great – I've got a job working at an old folks' home,' said Spider. 'The old people were a bit put out when they first saw me, so now I wear a woolly cap right down above my eyes so they can't see the tattoo on my forehead.' I wondered what they thought of the tattoos everywhere else on his face, but the lad meant well, and after all they would soon be removed.

Roy was in my room, reading the paper and drinking a glass of Canadian Club. 'I'll have one of those,' I said, and he promptly poured me a treble. We discussed Spider's visit, and he reminded me that today was to be Wilf's and my monthly soirée with Bodger Broom, the great Jarvis, the mad Scotsman Lewis Frame and the inimitable Sean Page, so I plundered the petty cash, in the knowledge that, though the meal would not be expensive, the drinks bill probably would be.

I was leaving for the afternoon court when an elderly lady with dyed blonde hair, black at the roots, and a heavily lined face walked into reception, wearing a faded coat and down-at-heel shoes – and was greeted by Spider with a shout: 'Mother!'

The lady simply replied, 'Michael,' and there was one of those pregnant pauses when the film goes into slow motion as they embraced and then started to cry. I urged them into the room set aside for them without introducing myself, closed the door, winked at Tracy and set off for court.

When I got back both Spider and his mother had gone, but apparently their reunion had been a great success. They'd gone out for the rest of the afternoon, and made plans for Spider to visit his mother in her new home in the south of England. The whole day had been a sizeable hit, the only blot on the landscape being the spectre of the court proceedings. Or at least, that's what I thought.

FOURTEEN

FITZGERALD FACES JAIL, AND SPIDER'S FOND FAREWELL

'Terence Jordan Fitzgerald to see you,' said Tracy. She was wearing a purple number with a tight-fitting top and pencil skirt, complemented by purple tights and purple shoes with brass buckles. As she left the room Fitzgerald turned to survey her rear appreciatively before he sat down in front of my desk and his concentration returned.

'To what do I owe this honour, Mr Fitzgerald?' I asked.

'The police've f-f-f-fetched me a summons for another tax disc, and when I was in court last time the f-f-foreign-looking magistrate told me if I came back he'd send me to jail.'

'Then why did you do it, Terry? You were only in court two days ago.'

'It just 'appened. I saw another tax disc, and picked it up.'

I looked at his charge sheet and realised the scale of his predicament. 'Yes, while it was still in a car. You've been charged with pinching that as well.'

'It's not f-f-f-fair,' he whined. 'I only borrowed it because I'd 'urt my f-f-foot and couldn't get 'ome. I didn't think me mate would mind.'

'But you don't have any insurance for this vehicle, do you?' I said. 'So you've got theft of a tax disc, taking a motor vehicle without consent, no insurance and – oh, what's this?' I said, noticing another piece of paper hiding in the envelope. 'Giving a false name to the police.'

'I gave him my mate's name, that's not f-f-f-false,' he said indignantly.

'It is to you, you twerp. What did you get when you were last in court?'

'F-f-f-fifty-pound fine.' Terry smiled. 'It's not as bad as I'm going to get this f-f-effing time.'

'Too f-f-f true,' I thought as I completed the documentation before sending him on his way.

'By the way,' said Terry, as he was leaving, 'Is she courting, your receptionist? I f-f-fancy her. Would she like a f-f-f-fair old night out? I'll take her to the dogs.'

'I'm sorry, Terry,' I said, 'But Tracy has a boyfriend.'

'Can he f-f-fight?'

'Why should he?'

'I just wondered, if it came down to a scrap.' Terry looked at me as though I were a Martian. The desire to solve all dilemmas with a fight, the heritage of Neanderthal man, was alive and well in Rotherham, and he simply didn't understand my eschewal of it.

As he was leaving Tracy walked in, and Terry winked at her. ''Ello, babe, do you like big boys?'

'No, do you?' she replied sharply.

'F-f-f-fancy that! She's quick, i'n't she?'

'Only if you're following me,' said Tracy, even more sharply. That floored Terry, and he gave it up as a bad job, but not before blowing her a kiss and informing me that she was 'playing hard to get'. He left whistling 'Mr Wonderful'.

'He likes you, Tracy,' I suggested.

'Thrilling,' she replied dismissively, and left the room whistling the theme tune from *The Great Escape*.

Wilf came in with the early edition newspaper, and pointed out that we had lost £5 because Monte's Revenge had come fourth at Haydock Park. As he flung the paper on my desk in disgust, a front-page headline stared me in the face: 'Local youth dies of drug overdose.'

I picked up the paper and read on.

Twenty-one-year-old found dead in flat. Police say the death is being treated as suspicious.

Michael Wellington McIver was found unconscious last night by his landlady. Police were contacted and he was taken to hospital but certified dead on arrival. The police have asked for anyone with information to contact any police station.

Just at that moment the phone rang.

'Hello, Mr Smith, DI Lightowler. I'm ringing about Michael Wellington McIver.'

'What happened?' I asked, in shock. 'I've just read the paper.'

'Well... I'll call round, if I may?'

'Yes, certainly. I'm going out in half an hour, so is there any chance ...?'

DI Lightowler interrupted me. 'I'll come now.'

'Thank you for seeing me, Mr Smith,' he said politely, when Sheila showed him in a few moments later. 'I'm involved in the McIver death investigation, and I wondered if you might be able to help me with some enquiries.'

'If I can,' I said. 'What do you want to know?'

'Well,' continued Lightowler, looking around the room making a mental note of its contents, 'I've been unable to contact McIver's mother. She lives in Northampton, but she's not at home, and I'm told she's staying with friends in this area with a view to meeting her son.'

'So she doesn't know, then?' I asked.

'Not unless she's read the paper or found out from some other source. Do you have a contact address?'

'I've got it in one of my notebooks, I think. I'll look.'

As I set about searching through a mass of papers, Lightowler inspected my certificates on the wall. 'Funny job, this one,' he said quizzically.

'Yes?' I said. 'The papers said you were treating it as suspicious. What happened?'

'Well, I shouldn't really be divulging information, but as you were his solicitor – he got hold of some heroin and took too much of it... looks like an overdose.' He stared at me intently, and my expression must have given me away, because he asked, 'You don't think it was anything else, do you, Mr Smith?'

'I can't give you anything but my own suspicions,' I said carefully. 'But Spider was off drugs. He'd tested negative for nearly four months now. And he was working, seeing his probation officer regularly, and had just been reunited with his mother. Everything was finally going for him. He was happy.'

'But these druggies can't pack it in,' Lightowler argued. 'They often promise great things, and some of them can keep off it for a day or so, but sooner or later they're bang at it again. I take it you don't accept that, Mr Smith?' he asked, noticing my reaction again.

'No, I don't. It just doesn't stack up. I can't see any reason for him to return to drugs, unless...' I paused momentarily to consider my idea.

Lightowler, his interest aroused, faced me with his eyes sparking in anticipation. 'Unless what, Mr Smith?' he asked.

'Well, I know he was frightened of the drug dealers who'd been using him, and had had to be rehoused to get out of their sights.'

Lightowler shook his head dismissively. 'So they probably found him and flogged him some more dope, and because he'd been off it for a while he took more than was wise. I don't exactly have a great deal to work on. No one seems to have seen him that day, there are no witnesses to any visitors he may or may not have had, so we're left with the simple conclusion that it was an overdose, for whatever reason.'

'I don't doubt that it was an overdose, but I'm concerned about how he came to take it,' I countered, rising to his bait.

'Are you suggesting that somebody killed him?' said the Inspector in mock indignation.

'I just don't believe he would have taken it of his own volition.'

'Well, as you know, Mr Smith, we can't prosecute on gut feelings.'

'Of course, Inspector,' I said, 'but you asked me my opinion, and I gave it. If you weren't prepared to listen you shouldn't have asked. Here's his mother's number. Look, maybe it would come better from me. No disrespect, but I have at least met her once, and she knows about me.'

The inspector thought for a minute before replying. 'Yes, if you like. It's a job less for me, and not a pleasant one at that. But would you ask her to ring me on this number?' he asked, passing me a card.

As he turned to leave, he said as if it were a casual afterthought, 'By the way, you don't know the names of these drug dealers, do you?'

I had my own suspicions of an obnoxious character with a red sports car, a man called Cusack whom I'd met when I first met Spider, but suspicions were all they were. 'No, I was never told, I'm afraid.'

'No, I suppose he kept it to himself,' said the inspector. 'I'll check through his files and see what I can come up with. If I find anything I'll let you know. Well, I'll be off then. No doubt our paths will cross again,' he said knowingly, and with that he was gone. He was the sort of man you couldn't help but dislike.

Wilf came back in. 'Who was that?' he asked. 'He saw me holding the glass of whisky, and looked as if he wanted to analyse it, and me as well.'

'Well, it's a good job you're not driving, as he's probably waiting outside. He's a policeman.'

'Ah, I thought he was,' said Wilf. 'He had that look about him... Sad about poor old Spider. The girls are quite upset. And after he'd just seen his mum again, too. Does she know?'

'No,' I replied.

'Who's telling her then?' asked Wilf. I didn't reply, just looked at him. 'Oh no! Rather you than me, old chap,' and Wilf sympathetically.

As soon as he left the office, I dialled the phone number in my notebook, which was answered almost immediately. The voice on the other end of the phone was Mrs McIver's friend, who promised to pass on my message that Mrs McIver should call to see me that afternoon on an urgent matter, and a little before five thirty she arrived.

I had a small glass of whisky before I went to collect her, and as I showed her into my room I noticed how much brighter she looked than last time. She had had her roots touched up, and was wearing a smart new coat and a new pair of shoes, because I could see the still clean price label on the sole of the right foot. Before I could speak, she began to tell me of her exciting reunion and her plans for her own and her son's future.

I never did get the chance to speak. There's something strange about bad news: I'm not sure whether it's body language or facial expressions, but it seems to seep out without any words. She suddenly paused, stared into my eyes, and said gravely, 'It's Michael, isn't it?'

I took a deep breath, since there was no easy way to tell her that her son was dead; the bond between mother and son is unique, no matter how the relationship has foundered in the past. Again, it was almost as if she had some premonition of what I was about to say. Before I could begin my sentence, she had already realised what my reluctance was concealing.

'He's dead, isn't he?'

I nodded, and waited for a response. While Sheila brought in a cup of tea (she had an almost prescient sense of when such gestures were needed), Mrs McIver maintained a blank expression, almost as if she'd been paralysed. I reached for the whisky bottle in my cupboard, and poured her a glass.

After a second or two Mrs McIver came out of her trance and politely declined the drink, saying that she had agreed with Michael she would give up alcohol in return for his giving up drugs. She asked for an explanation, and I did my best to placate her with my opinion. Then, slowly but not reluctantly, she got up and left the room without speaking. I followed her to the top of the stairs, offering my assistance in any way, and she forced a smile, but just went out and closed the door behind her.

The tree-lined drive into the crematorium had been a solemn pathway for many cortèges over the years, and would no doubt continue so throughout my lifetime. An official, wearing black with pinstripe trousers, was walking to his office with a sprightly gait. 'What a job,' I thought. 'I wonder if he thinks about his final party?'

I sat in the back row on the left, watching intently as some seven or eight mourners listened to the words of the Reverend Blanchard. With consummate courtesy, the good reverend spoke of the efforts Spider had made to come to terms with his addiction and all his other problems. He was obviously doing his best to find something appropriate to say to a small gathering of people whom he had probably never seen before. Mrs McIver, consumed by grief and, I suspect, feeling more than a little guilt, sat at the front being consoled by a woman I assumed was her friend, her cheeks flushed, her eyes reddened with crying. I noticed the familiar faces of Spider's probation officer and social worker, and there was also a young man of about Spider's age. Sitting in the opposite back corner to mine was Detective Inspector Lightowler.

The service was short but poignant, and when it ended the

gathering left to the eerie sound of the sixties pop song 'Kites' by Simon Duprey and the Big Sound. There was one funeral car, and I stood in the doorway and watched Mrs McIver and her friend drive away from the crematorium steps, up the long winding path to the large gates, until they were out of sight. Within seconds, a new cortège for some other unfortunate entered, and the whole sequence started again.

'This is everybody's destiny,' said Lightowler grimly, disturbing my thoughts.

'Yes, it's not much to look forward to, is it?' I said. 'And it's even worse when it ends like this. What brings you here, Mr Lightowler?' I asked.

'Just thought I'd pay my respects, so to speak, and see who turned up.'

I had absolutely no doubt he had come to see who turned up, but I wasn't too sure about his first claim. Yet it intrigued me that he had attended at all; I wondered if he'd taken on board some of my comments.

'If you hear anything on the grapevine,' said Lightowler, 'doubtless you'll keep me informed.'

'Of course,' I said. 'You know my views.'

Lightowler forced a half-smile before striding off in the direction of the car park, and after a moment or two I walked up the long winding path myself in the same direction, struck by the tranquillity of the area and the tidiness of the flower beds, which would hardly ever be noticed in this place.

As I drove off, I saw a red sports car parked on its own at the far side of the car park, with an open view of the gates and the chapel itself. I couldn't make out the occupants, who seemed to be reluctant to show themselves – or perhaps it was just my imagination. I shivered without explanation as I drove through the main gates, to arrive back in Rotherham in time for the afternoon court, where I was to represent a drug supplier whose case was first in the list.

FIFTEEN

RETURN OF THE PRODIGAL

'Why should I plead guilty when I haven't done it!' shouted Fifi DuPont, the Sheffield prostitute and thief who was denying being a Sheffield prostitute and thief. 'What would I want with a Black and Decker drill?' she protested.

'The mind boggles,' I thought, as I listened to a tirade of complaint and aggression.

'The last thing I want you to do is to plead guilty to something you haven't done, but I do ask you to consider the evidence of the store detective,' I put in at last. 'He says he saw you pick up the deodorant stick and push it down your cleavage.'

'He didn't see that at all,' she persisted angrily. 'In that case I'd've had three tits! Come off it, get real – he couldn't even see me from where he was, unless he can see round corners, and he can't do that, not while he has a hole in his arse.' Miss DuPont had a nice turn of phrase, but as she continued to vent her spleen I couldn't help wondering what the point of studying all those law books had been, only to be told that Derek Morgan, the store detective, might well find his anal canal sealing itself with the passage of time. 'He ought to go fuck himself,' she concluded.

'I just wonder why he'd say he saw it if it wasn't true. What has he got against you?'

'He doesn't like me. I saw him watching me... Dirty bastard!'

There was no point in arguing with Fifi in that mood, because as a pathological liar she had talked herself into believing her innocence, and to push the point further would only antagonise her. It was time to back off and try again another day. It's always hard for a client to admit guilt, particularly if they've just spent time trying to persuade you to the contrary.

Fifi – or Janet Wadkin, as her birth certificate and the DSS knew her – was an unusual woman, moulded by the path on which life had wastefully led her, given her high IQ. Placed in a home at the age of eleven, she had her first child at thirteen and at fourteen started 'on the game', which she had played ever since. At thirty-six going on sixty, with her best years behind her and staring oblivion helplessly in the face, she was a living example of the old maxim: 'A person who cannot trust is a person who himself (or in Fifi's case, herself) cannot be trusted.' But dishonest and foul-mouthed as she was, I couldn't help feeling sorry for her; she was one of life's casualties without even really knowing it. She was tall, about five foot nine, with dyed blonde hair whose roots were usually just beginning to show. The mandatory bright red lipstick and dark eyeshadow of her profession gave her an almost clown-like appearance. Her eyelids had begun to sag over dead eyes – the giveaway of so many prostitutes – but her high cheekbones and dimpled chin were still attractive, and an almost obscenely short mini-skirt revealed shapely legs draped with fishnet tights.

To re-establish myself in her eyes before she decided I was 'just like the rest, always ready to criticise', I changed tack. 'I've been told you have a high IQ,' I said. 'Why didn't you stay on at school?'

'I was brought up in a home and I had to leave,' she replied, more calmly. 'So I got a flat and went to work on the streets. It was the easiest thing to do, and the money's good. What is this, *Twenty Questions*?' Her eyes narrowed. 'I was wrong, of course, but it's too late now,' she said contemplatively. 'I couldn't change if I wanted to.'

'What about your father?'

'He was nice, but Mum kicked him out when I was seven, and

that's when the uncles started to come. Don't look innocent, you know what I mean. Well, she had to live somehow, didn't she? He came for me once in the home, but they wouldn't let me out. He said he'd come back, but he never did, not until I was about twenty. I'd moved around, you see, and changed my name to duck the police and the DSS, which didn't make it easy for him. And I didn't want him to see I was on the game proper, so I pretended not to be in. It broke my heart, but what would he have thought? That poor man. But I can't put back the clock,' she said dejectedly. 'That's why I never talk about it, it upsets me.'

For the first time, I thought I saw the glint of a tear, a hint that she was human after all. 'But he must be sixty now?'

'Sixty-four,' she replied. 'Sixty-five on Christmas Eve, to be exact. But he moved away, I heard, somewhere down south. I'll admit I've wondered about him – every single day,' she added softly.

Having touched her suppressed conscience, I wouldn't be deterred. 'Why don't you find him?'

'What would I say? Hello, Dad, I'm a prostitute and have convictions to prove it. Oh, and I'm a thief and a liar as well, and I have a drink problem… Don't ask me any more. You know, I'd think better of you if you offered me a drink. Have you got any whisky?'

'Okay,' I replied. 'One tot with my compliments.'

'Thanks, Steve,' she said, taking the glass carefully so as not to spill any of its contents. She drank it in one gulp, placing it on the end of my desk with panache. 'I'm off now. We've finished, haven't we?'

'I suppose so, but I want you to think about your plea.'

'You want me to go guilty, don't you?'

'I want you to put the best case you can without sticking your neck out, because if you fight and it goes wrong you'll get a heavier sentence, which in your case could mean prison, and then you'd blame me,' I said honestly.

She smiled, being bright enough to see I was advising her for the best. 'Can you get cannabis in prison, Steve?' she asked.

'There's not much you can't get in prison – except your freedom,' I said. 'But there are some funny women in there – you wouldn't like it.'

She smiled again, once again having taken the point. 'All this talk of prison and funny women is depressing. I'll see you in court, like they say.' She blew me a kiss, pushed back her hair and left the room.

That was the cue for Sheila to come in with the post. One letter stood out, because I recognised the writing, and we'd had to pay an excess charge to the Post Office since the sender hadn't put a stamp on. Yes, it was a missive from Mr Albert Heptonstall, formerly of this parish.

I opened the envelope with care because, knowing Albert, there could be anything inside, unfolded the grand-looking letterhead of an expensive hotel, then read the contents.

Steve,

It's me, Albert. Ow are u? I'm all reet, Mother and others are all reet, likewise snake, dog, goat an' me pidgins – we're all all reet. Are u? I 'opc u are, cos then we're all all reet.

But Dad's not all reet. 'E wants to come back, can't settle, so we're floggin' the pidgins an' comin' 'ome. Dad's spoke to t'counsil, an' we're takin' an exchange. Tha'll nivver guess – we're kummin back to t'same 'ouses! That's great, innit?

Anyroad, it's next munth, an' we're 'avin' a party and want thee to kum. Dad said tha'll be pleased, so I think tha should no fust. See thee next munth.

Albert.

PS Grandad's all reet too, but Dad's piles are ruff.

I couldn't help but smile, and in fact I was pleased – apart from

Jack's piles, of course. Unrequited joy would be an overstatement, but since they had been about half my criminal practice, I would actually be glad to see the Heptonstall clan back in Rotherham – and the incredible stroke of luck that had them returning to the same two council houses they had occupied prior to their departure looked remarkably like fate.

The party they organised about a month after their return was also a remarkable occasion. Bunting was draped from house to house – the flags had a white background, and close scrutiny revealed the words 'Closing Down Sale' in red in the middle of each. Tables were set out in the street holding sandwiches, pork pies, sausage rolls and similar delicacies, but one brightly coloured table outside Jack's house included a vat of the most awful-looking foodstuff I'd ever seen.

Jack's wife Madge greeted me like a long-lost friend, enthusi- astically pumping my hand with a grip that made me wince. 'It's good to see you again, Steve,' she said, handing over a plate with the odious-looking contents. 'Try my whelk stew. Our Albert's favourite, it is. 'E loves whelks, particularly fried up with a bit of mash.'

Noting my attempt to cover my revulsion, she persisted, 'Just try one, Steve, an' see what yer think. If tha thinks it's crap, spit it over Billy One-Leg's wall,' she smiled, displaying a ridge of gum remarkable for its want of teeth. There could be no doubt that she was Albert's mother.

To avoid causing offence, I took one of the ghoulish-looking objects and plunged it into my mouth, pretended to chew it, making noises of culinary satisfaction, but when she wasn't look- ing I surreptitiously flicked it over the fence into Billy One-Leg's garden, then moved off rather quickly on hearing him shout a complaint.

Jack appeared, wearing a red-and-white Caribbean shirt, green- and-white football shorts, and a pair of hiking boots with white sports socks draped over their tops. He passed me a paper plate and urged me to fill it with whelks, but I declined politely and made for the chicken legs, beautifully stacked in a pyramid. I took two, plus a dripping breadcake, and was eating my last mouthful when Jack engaged me in conversation.

'What do you think to t'whelk stew, Steve?' asked Jack, seeking praise.

'Very nice, Jack. Unusual, but very tasty.'

'Aye, it is that,' said Jack. 'Just a minute.' He turned to Madge and asked earnestly, 'Madge, 'ave you seen me pile ointment?'

'Tha what, Jack?' she asked.

Jack shouted at the top of his voice, 'Me pile ointment!' A number of guests turned in bewilderment, and I hastily replaced two grapes on the dish I'd just taken them from.

'Next to the Fiery Jack in the bathroom,' said Madge.

'Right,' said Jack, 'I'm going upstairs to put some on. I can't sit down reet!'

As he moved off, Madge shouted after him, 'Be careful! They're in the same colour pots.'

Then Albert appeared, eating what seemed to be the remnants of a leg of lamb. 'Eh up, Steve,' he said, 'Thanks for coming. Does tha want a whelk?'

'Hello, Albert,' I said. 'I'll pass on the whelks and have one of those custard tarts,' pointing to an array of confectionery. Albert reached for one, took off the silver foil, and handed it to me.

'You ill-mannered little bugger,' said his grandmother. 'You should always offer food by handing over the plate.'

'Righto, Grandma,' said Albert, took the half-eaten custard out of my hand and placed it on a paper plate, and handed it back with a grin.

'Ee, that lad,' said Grandma Heptonstall. 'What can you do with him?'

I was then treated to a flagon of a sickly looking substance Jack had been fermenting over a period of time, from an idea he had picked up from *The Great Escape*, where the American prisoners-of-war had found a way of making hooch by distilling potatoes. It occurred to me that he should have a licence to do so, but I didn't have the energy to try to explain that, and I must confess the brew had a certain *je ne sais quoi*.

Then I was introduced to the local council housing manager's representative, a nice middle-aged bloke, tall and thin with a black moustache and wire-rimmed glasses, a dead ringer for Doctor Crippen, known as Zed, who explained that he had turned up out of pure relief that Jack had ceased to phone him every day. He wore a tweed sports coat, cavalry-twill trousers, and thick-soled shoes, and carried a brown briefcase that had seen better days – if you had to pick his profession, you would certainly guess immediately that he came from the town hall. I began chatting to him, but after he had dealt in detail with the problems of the Rotherham housing office we seemed to have exhausted all topics of conversation, so I moved on.

Just then Jack came back, clearly in extreme discomfort. 'I'm walking like bleedin' John Wayne,' he grimaced. 'Tha don't ever want these piles,' he continued. 'They make tha life a misery. Madge, where's that bloody ointment?'

'I told you, in the bathroom cupboard. But not now; it's time for a song.'

'Aw reet, then,' said Jack. 'Where's our Venn?'

Venn, the second youngest sibling, had a pronounced stutter, which disappeared when he sang in an unusually harmonious voice. Announcing his song took a long time, owing to his affliction, but when he broke into the strains of 'Unchained Melody' I was amazed at how moving it was. He received tremendous applause, together with shouts of 'More!' from Dr Crippen from the council, by now on his third glass of punch. Venn followed with an excellent rendition of 'Why Must I be a Teenager in Love?', and everyone joined in the refrain. Another rousing reaction from the audience prompted a third song, the Martha and the Vandellas classic 'Dancin' in the Street', urged on by an extremely tipsy Dr Crippen, now up to number seven. The whole street entered into the spirit of the occasion – 'It doesn't matter what you wear, just as long as you are there... Ev'rywhere around the world... La-la-la, la-la-la-la... dancin' in the street.' Towards the end, Dr Crippen treated us to his version of the twist, which ended when he fell to the floor and his stomach rejected Jack's punch and the whelks.

'He's not a bad lad, that kid from the council,' said Jack, 'but he can't hold his liquor or his whelks.' I nodded impassively as Madge tended to Zed by offering him black coffee and another whelk, which induced him to vomit again.

Jack sat down (carefully) to give me an in-depth analysis of his health problem, which he described as the 'grapes of wrath': I momentarily confused Steinbeck's famous book with three witch-es from Goole.

'It's no good,' he said. 'I'm going to 'ave to put some of that cream on,' and disappeared.

I was just wondering whether to talk to someone else or leave when a young girl appeared. About sixteen and beautifully dressed, she was extremely pretty, with bright blue eyes and a beautiful complexion, and quickly became the centre of attention as she tiptoed to Albert, put her hands over his eyes and called, 'Guess who?' in beautifully modulated received pronunciation. From her expression, it was obvious that she was smitten with him, which I couldn't for the life of me understand.

'Oh, 'ello Caroline,' said Albert despondently, 'What are you doin' 'ere?'

'I've come for your party. Your mum invited me. Do you want to go for a walk? The park's beautiful at this time of year.'

Albert looked at me, and then at the heavens, for inspiration. 'I can't,' he said, finding it. 'It's me dad's party. Come back another day.'

But Madge had heard, and intervened. "Ello, Caroline, thanks for coming. Our Albert will go up to the park with you a little later, won't you, Albert?'

Albert glared at her, but Madge's wrists were thicker than his, so he nodded reluctantly. 'Oh, good,' said Caroline. 'I must say, I enjoyed Venn's singing. He's got an excellent voice, and it's remarkable how the stutter disappears once he starts to sing. I bet you're a good singer too, Albert,' she continued.

'Ah,' said Albert.

'Not as good as he is at conversation,' I thought.

Caroline went into the house, striding over the now recumbent Dr Crippen in the process, and I asked, 'Is that the new girlfriend, then, Albert?'

'No,' he snapped. 'She's just an 'anger-on, a bloody nuisance. She's always trying to get me to take her out. She asked me to go the library the other day. What for? It's full of books.'

'Do you mean to tell me you don't like her? But she's gorgeous.'

'Ah, but it's not so much 'er as who she is. Look at 'er clobber. She's got money, ain't she? I can't cope wi' that. She speaks French an' all. 'Ow could I cope with 'er folks – I can't even speak English!'

'But you're as good as anyone else,' I tried.

'I can't compete. What would 'er folks think about me crappy clothes an' big boots?' he said disconsolately.

'She likes you. Why don't you take her out?'

'What with? Where to?'

Albert, I realised, was ashamed of his inadequacies. Before I could put matters right, Grandad Heptonstall, a sweet old man but not in full control of his faculties, tugged at my trouser leg from his wheelchair. 'Are you the undertaker? Is it a cremation?'

I said, 'No, Grandad. I've come to see your son Jack.'

"E's not booking my funeral, is 'e?'

'No, Grandad,' said Albert. 'Luckily tha's not dead yet.'

'I want plenty of flowers. I'm going to be cremated,' said the old man forcefully.

'Sooner than you think,' interjected Jack. 'Stop bothering Mr Smith, 'e 'asn't come 'ere to listen to talk like that.' He put his arm around his father. 'Come on now, your programme's on, so I'll take you in and get you a brown ale.'

'Thanks, son,' said the old man, holding out his hand to me. We shook, and as he wheeled him away Jack shook his head. 'Silly old bugger,' he said. 'It comes to us all one day.'

The most enormous man I'd ever seen, almost seven feet tall and I'd guess over twenty-five stone, rather like one of those giant American wrestlers, was wearing tracksuit bottoms and a T-shirt, which accentuated his giant frame. He had black curly hair, the look of a gypsy, and hands like malt shovels. Despite his dimensions he was also slightly effeminate, with an oddly high-pitched voice which didn't fit his build at all, although I doubted anyone would dare tell him so. Introduced to me as 'Big Percy', he nearly lifted me off the floor when we shook hands.

'Tha's Jack's mate the solicitor, ain't thee?'

'Well, I know him very well, yes.'

''E's aw reet, is Jack. Does tha want to buy a whippet?'

A bit taken aback by the offer, I said, 'No, thanks, I've already got a dog.'

'Well, if tha ivver wants a good whippet, come and see me. I know all there is to know about whippets,' said Big Percy, and moved off in search of food. It was like the end of an eclipse when his huge body moved out of the sunlight.

'He's a big bugger, Jack,' I said.

'Ay, he's big,' said Jack, 'but 'e's a nice bloke. 'E'll do some arm-wrestling later on; 'e's never been beaten, the cock of Yorkshire. 'E drives one of them Harley Davidsons with the big thick tyres on it. The dog's bollocks, it is.'

At that moment I caught sight of Caroline standing alone and decided to engage her in conversation, since I thought it fascinating that a well-spoken and quite beautiful girl would have an interest in someone like Albert. I introduced myself, and was surprised to find that she knew of me.

'My father's told me about you, and of course Albert talks about no one else.'

'Oh, really?' I replied, wondering in what context. It wasn't clear to me whether she knew about Albert's chequered past, so I chose my words carefully. 'How did you meet him, Caroline?'

'At the animal sanctuary. He's absolutely brilliant with animals, and everybody there says he's a genius.'

'Oh, he's that all right,' I said. 'I once watched him control the geese at his allotment, and it was incredible.'

'Exactly,' beamed Caroline. 'He's so kind and gentle that all the animals respond to him.'

I wondered whether to tell her about the time he came to my office and tried to spear my fish, but to be fair, that was long in the past. 'How long have you known him?' I asked.

'Well, he goes to the animal sanctuary nearly every day, and I'm doing a project there for my exams – I want to be a vet. His family are all really nice to me, especially his mum, and his dad's a real character, isn't he? I had tea at their house the other day.'

'Did you really?' I asked. It was obvious she knew nothing of Albert's criminal past, and I certainly wasn't going to tell her. 'And you said your father knows me? What does he do, Caroline?'

'He's in the CID – Inspector Lightowler.'

I choked on the lethal-tasting punch I was sipping, spraying it over the unfortunate Billy One-Leg. Caroline continued, blithely unawares, 'And he's really interested to meet Albert, so I'm going to take him home for tea soon.'

I nearly choked again at the thought of Albert arriving at Inspector Lightowler's house and being questioned about his career prospects, and I realised that I somehow felt protective towards him.

When Caroline moved away to speak to Madge, I rejoined Albert, intending to sound him out further about this awkward relationship. Before I could open my mouth, there was an almighty bellow from indoors. 'Arghhh, bleeding 'ell! Madge...! Madge, bleedin' 'ell, me arse is on fire!'

I recalled Madge's instructions to Jack earlier, and deduced that he'd mixed up the pile ointment and the Fiery Jack. It seemed like a good moment to make a discreet exit...

SIXTEEN

ADIEU DEXTER PAGE, SO LONG MRS MOTT

Gerry Woodward had fallen foul of one of life's great tragedies, namely a broken marriage. Unfortunately, owing to an acrimonious divorce there were problems with access to his seven-year-old son Scott, who was the apple of his eye. This is one of the frequent side-effects in the game of 'getting even with my spouse'. Gerry was a good father, with a university degree, and had just started work in the fairly new field of computers, but though he loved Norma, his former wife, they simply could not get on. An aggravating feature was that Norma was an alcoholic, and regrettably Gerry was going the same way.

Norma refused to let him see his son, so Gerry had come to see me with a view to pursuing a case for access, something easier said than done. Since Norma chose to be awkward we had to fight it out in the courts, where Gerry won the case and was awarded 'specified access', which meant that he saw his son at certain times on certain days. Then Norma tragically contracted cancer of the liver, and died early that year.

Social services had become involved, because of Gerry's own decline into drink, accelerated by all the stress, and because they felt that his one-roomed flat was unsuitable to bring up a young child in. There was a hearing before the magistrates to determine whether the child should be taken into care, and I had had a meeting with Gerry to try to sort out reasonable accommodation, which would help our case. Unfortunately when I met him he was drunk, apparently having great difficulty coming to terms with his wife's death and the whole issue of his son's care, so I had to suspend the meeting. I was busily trying to pick up the threads of his application when Pagey telephoned.

'Now then, old bean, what's the state of play, eh?'

'Not bad, Pagey. I've got plenty on, but I'm not complaining.'

'Had a spot of bad news, old bean,' said Pagey briskly. 'Uncle Dexter snuffed it.'

'Oh, I'm sorry to hear that, Pagey. He was a great chap.' I knew Dexter, having attended one or two of the great boozing sessions that he and Pagey indulged in. He had been a distinguished character, still with a full head of snow-white hair in his seventies, who had worn expensive suits which gave him the air of a medical man, although his business had been land agency. Despite a succession of long-term girlfriends, he'd managed to avoid the altar with all of them. Virtually all of his relatives were Methodists who disapproved of alcohol and, consequently, of both Dexter and Sean, who they considered was following in his uncle's reprehensible footprints, and had had little or no contact with either of them.

'Certainly was, old man, a great sport, a fine boozer and a gentleman. The trouble and strife doted on him. She's very upset.'

'Yes, I imagine,' I said sympathetically.

'Well, I'm ringing to tell you, old bean, that the funeral's at three pm tomorrow, preceded by old Dexter's lying-in at my house. The hearse is due at two fifteen to take him away to have the flowers put on the coffin, then they'll come back for everybody else at two forty-five, and off to the church and the crem.' Pagey's matter-of-fact attitude was typical. I had absolutely no doubt he was moved by the loss of his uncle, but he was always one to sort out the practicalities. 'Are you coming for a pre-cremation swig?'

'Yes,' I replied. My case the following afternoon had been cancelled because the defendant had sent in a sick-note, and it was fitting that I should pay my respects. 'I'll do that. What time do you want me?'

'Oh,' said Pagey, 'get here about a quarter to two, then we've an hour before the Methodists arrive.' Naturally the disapproving cousins had been invited to the funeral, and would apparently be attending from their various homes in the south of England.

'Very good,' I replied. 'I'll see you then.'

I set off after the close of the morning court – prudently making use of the local taxi firm, run by a friend and client Geoff Taylor – and arrived at about 1.15pm to find Bodger, Lewis Frame and the great Jarvis already drinking Newcastle Brown Ale fortified by the odd spot of brandy. I was given a glass of each, and after the usual salutations Pagey invited us all into the front room to pay our last respects. There lay Dexter with his arms folded, looking serene set against the white satin-lined coffin.

'Not a bad-looking old stick is he, even now? It's a shame he missed my birthday, we were in for a really big session,' said Pagey, and proceeded to wax lyrical in his inimitable manner, telling us various stories from Dexter's past. Then he administered fresh drinks to us all and we honoured Dexter with a toast.

'Here's to old Dexter – entrepreneur, first-division boozer, and all-round good egg!' Pagey proclaimed.

As we all muttered our 'Hear, hears,' he put his glass down on the corner of the coffin and said proudly, 'He'd be pleased that you lot have turned up. It should be a really good send-off for the old salt – God bless you, Dexter, old man,' he said, gesticulating expansively towards the deceased.

Unfortunately, in the heat of the moment he had forgotten his precariously perched pint, and inevitably there was contact. The glass fell inwards, covering the satin lining and Dexter's shock of white hair with Newcastle Brown Ale.

We all gasped. Pagey uttered some extremely vulgar words and, as nearly at a loss as I've ever seen him, cried, 'Christ, now what do we do?' before burying his head in his hands.

Disarmed of criticism by his obvious distress, the rest of us looked at each other, then gathered around the coffin to survey the damage. Newcastle Brown is a gloriously rich, dark beer. Not surprisingly, when it comes into contact with white satin and white human hair, it leaves a substantial stain, a strong smell, and a pervasive stickiness. By now it was ten past two, and the funeral directors were due in five minutes. Luckily the guests weren't expected for half an hour after that: the Methodists probably wouldn't be too impressed by a beer-swilled Dexter.

'I know!' said Pagey, with the inspiration of desperation. 'If we can dry his hair and the satin, we can chuck on some talcum powder to cover the discoloration.' He disappeared upstairs, returning within seconds with a hairdryer and a tin of lavender-scented talcum. 'Lift his head up while I dry the back of his hair,' he ordered, looking at me.

'Bugger off,' I retorted.

'Come on, Smithy,' said Pagey, 'be a sport.'

'You must think I fell out of a tree. Not me. Ask Jarvis.'

'Sod off,' said Jarvis, 'I'm not doing it.'

'Oh, for Christ's sake, they'll be here in a minute,' said Pagey. 'You can't leave me to swing for this.'

'I'll do it,' said Bodger, and did. But then he complained in surprise, ''Is 'ead's cold!'

'It would be; he's dead,' I replied sarcastically.

Pagey did his best with the satin, and Bodger administered the talcum powder, smoothing it carefully over the beer marks, then Pagey then started drying Dexter's hair. The scene can only be imagined in one's wildest dreams. Bodger was holding Dexter's head up, I was supporting his left shoulder and Jarvis his right, while Pagey tried to dry his beer-anointed scalp.

In our frenzy, we hadn't heard the arrival of the undertaker – or, more importantly, of Dexter's Methodist relatives. The door sprang open to reveal Auntie Margaret – formerly of Hitler Youth – in mid-sentence: 'Sean, it's Aunt Margaret and Uncle Jeffrey, come to pay our respec...'

The silence seemed to last for ages, until it was broken by Pagey, saying breathlessly, 'Uncle Margaret and Aunt Jeffrey, how wonderful to see you again. Come in and say hello – I mean, goodbye – to Uncle Dexter. We were just, er... drying his hair.'

The next Thursday saw me suffering from the effects of one of our monthly soirées, at which Pagey had been down in the dumps, having been ostracised by the Methodist branch of his family after the chaos of the wake (Pagey and we Three Musketeers had even been barred from the funeral tea). I arrived at the office late and attempted to go through a stream of correspondence before setting out to deal with the morning's court. Mrs Mott, our remarkable cleaner, spotted that I had something of a hangover – perhaps the bags under my eyes, my pathetic moans, and the fact that I was drinking water by the jugful gave her a clue.

'You look under the weather, Mr Smith,' she said sympathetically.

'I've just got a bit of a headache, Mrs Mott. I'm afraid I had one over the eight last night.'

'More like eight over the eight,' said Mrs Mott. 'I'll fetch you some Alka Seltzer, and you drink it straight down, with a spoonful of honey in vinegar after – it's the best remedy in the world.'

Mrs Mott meant well and I had no wish to offend her, so I swallowed the two concoctions, the latter making me grimace enough to enter the National Gurning Championships.

'Not very nice, is it?' said Mrs Mott. 'All you've got to do now, Mr Smith, is to keep that down. It'll cure it in an hour. Don't drink any water while that vinegar settles.'

'But the after-taste, Mrs Mott...' I said pathetically.

'You'll have to put up with that. You'll know not to do it next time.' Medical practice according to Doctor Mott did not meet with my complete enthusiasm, but who was I to argue? I gathered my papers together and left for court.

Gerry Woodward was waiting at the street door. He had about three days' growth of beard, his hair was totally unkempt, and he reeked as though he had slept in a brewery – in fact he looked very similar to me.

'Now then, Gerry, what's the problem?' I asked.

'It's not good, Steve,' he said, his voice sounding as rough as he looked. 'Social services are going for an interim care order, and they seem to think the court'll grant it.'

'Well, if they do,' I replied, 'it only lasts for twenty-eight days before it has to be renewed, which will give you a month to get your act together.'

'How the bloody hell can I do that? Just look at the state of me. I've nowhere for him to live, I'm pissed every day, and quite frankly I'm losing the will.'

'Look Gerry, I'm late for court as it is, but if you'd like to come up there with me, when we get a break I'll buy you a cup of tea and we'll have a chat.'

'Okay,' said Gerry, 'I'll walk up with you.'

I had six cases to deal with that day, representing a variety of sins including shoplifters, carlifters and shirtlifters, with a couple of prostitutes thrown in for good measure. One of the girls claimed to be called Veronique LaTour, though according to her criminal record she was Mavis Juppe, born near Grimsby, and with about ten pages of convictions for minor theft and prostitution. She had been 'on the game' since her mid-teens, and whilst the record said that she was thirty, she looked considerably older. Her co-accused lady of the night was my old client Fifi DuPont, alias Janet Wadkin.

They had been picked up by the police outside the local nightclub and charged with soliciting, but were pleading not guilty, claiming that they were merely walking up and down outside the club, wait-ing for their boyfriends to pick them up. The prosecution said that they had been seen speaking to a number of young men, allegedly offering their services, and when they were arrested, both their bags were found to contain a strange electrical appliance together with various packets of condoms. The defendants, on the other hand, claimed they were only asking the men if they'd seen their boy-friends, and that they always carried condoms to cover all eventuali-ties. The trouble was that they looked like prostitutes, and when they gave their evidence I feared they would also sound like them. I took them into the rat-hole to discuss the case, and suggested that perhaps a court might find it difficult to believe their version of events.

'Are tha trying to say we luk guilty?' said Veronique in a broad South Yorkshire accent, without even a hint of French.

'Well,' I said apologetically, 'the court will look at all the sur-rounding evidence and put two and two together, and I think they'll make four.'

'Well, they ought to be shot wi' shit,' said Miss DuPont.

'That wouldn't get us out of this particular difficulty, I'm afraid.'

'We still want to fight it, Steve,' said Veronique. 'There's nowt wrong wi' carrying a few johnnies, is there? So we're both not guilty, sod 'em!'

There was no real answer to that, so I just nodded my agree-ment and we marched into court.

'What have you got for us today, Steve?' asked Keith Copley, the court clerk.

'Three pleas, two adjournments, and Miss LaTour and Miss DuPont, who insist that they're pleading not guilty to soliciting.'

'The court won't like that,' said Copley. 'Do you want to call them first?'

'No, they're outside drumming up a bit of trade. I'll get rid of my other adjournments first, if I may?'

'As you please,' said Copley, just as the three magistrates walked into court. The chairman was the man known locally as the Lord Chief Justice, with whom I had crossed swords many times in the past. The Lord Chancellor had recently written to all the courts that there were too many adjournments, which was causing massive delays in the legal system and increasing the legal aid bill: it was inevitable that the Lord Chief Justice would refuse any applications to adjourn, particularly from me.

Sure enough, even though Neil Franklin of the CPS raised no objection to my two adjournments (which were necessary for proper legal reasons), the Lord Chief Justice tried to refuse them, and Keith Copley had to intervene to point out that they were in the interests of justice. It was clear that the Lord Chief Justice was annoyed at having to grant them, and seemed to think that it was all my fault. That's the way it was, and always will be, in court life – he disliked me, and would do everything in his power to cause me problems.

We then called Mesdames LaTour and DuPont into the courtroom, where Fifi lied about both her address and date of birth, and was followed by Veronique.

'What is your full name, please?'

'Veronique Maisie LaTour, name changed by deed poll.'

'Very good,' said Keith. 'And your address, please, madam?'

'Forty-two Loughborough Rise, Wath, and I'm in most evenings after eleven.'

The observers in the public gallery laughed, but Keith pretended to miss the point, and asked her date of birth.

'A gentleman shouldn't ask a lady her date of birth,' said Veronique.

'Oh, get on with it,' said the Lord Chief Justice. 'You're charged with an offence, and you are obliged to answer the court's questions.'

'I may be charged with an offence,' said Veronique indignantly, 'but as I have not yet been convicted I believe that this court must treat me as an innocent person. If you've no respect for me, at least you can show some respect for the court and the people's rights.'

'Well said!' I thought.

The Lord Chief Justice spluttered. 'Will you speak to your

client, Mr Smith?'

'What about, sir?' I asked, feigning bewilderment.

'Her conduct, Mr Smith, her conduct! And watch your own whilst you do it.'

I spoke to Veronique, who giggled as though I'd told her a joke. The Lord Chief Justice, obviously believing I had done just that, shouted, 'MR SMITH! Are you quite ready?'

'Yes, sir, thank you.'

'Well, get on with it!'

Keith took the defendants' pleas.

'Not guilty,' said Fifi.

'Not guilty, most certainly,' said Veronique.

The Lord Chief Justice asked if we could proceed there and then, but Keith had to tell him there would have to be an adjournment to enable the police to bring the witnesses to court. I couldn't resist saying, 'May it please you, sir, I am in a position to proceed today, but if the court requires an adjournment I won't object.' I smiled as I sat down, thinking, 'Take that, shitface!' and the Lord Chief spluttered some more.

There was a tap on my shoulder, and when I turned, Veronique said in a stage whisper, 'That's put one up 'im!'

'Yes, I rather think it has,' I replied.

Keith Copley winked at me and I bowed graciously before leaving the court. As I walked out into the court corridor, Veronique nipped my bottom quite firmly and announced for all to hear that I had a 'nice arse'. The Lord Chief Justice didn't say a word. She then embarrassed me by putting a contraceptive in my top pocket, saying that I should save it for later and she would give me a ring and 'fix a date'.

I beat a hasty retreat to the solicitors' room to recount the story to some of the other solicitors. A young man called Julian Tierney, the son of my former mentor and employer George Tierney, was working in the court for his father. He thought the contraceptive episode was amusing, so I threw it at him, then went back into court to deal with my other cases.

When I returned, the room was empty. I put on my coat and reached into my pocket for my keys, and was stopped in my tracks by something oily and soft coming into contact with the palm of my hand. I drew it out. Tierney had opened the contraceptive, unrolled it and placed it in the pocket of my mackintosh.

'You bastard,' I said aloud, just as a WRVS lady came in to collect cups. She caught sight of the offending item, cleared her throat loudly, retrieved the cups and left tutting.

'Bloody marvellous!' I thought. The story would now be the talk of the tea-room and travel like wildfire. That old Rotherham maxim, 'If you throw enough shit about, everyone will get a bit' would apply, ensuring that henceforth I would be known as the 'Johnny-Toting Brief'. The least I could do was to return the compliment, so I put the rubber into Julian's coat pocket – or so I thought.

I was telling my friend David Walters the story when Julian walked in, picked up his coat, bade farewell and left. Immediately there was a major problem; he had not picked up the coat with the contraceptive. However, before I got a chance to move, a visiting magistrate from Sheffield came in to collect the offending garment, and we watched in horror as he put it on. To make matters worse, he was joined by his wife and the Lord Chief Justice. The immortal words 'Oh shit' came to mind as I inched towards the door, intending to make myself scarce.

Just as I got there, the visiting magistrate announced that he had found the meeting at Rotherham most stimulating and would have liked to stay longer, but he had another appointment elsewhere. 'I'd like to take this opportunity of thanking everyone at the court for their hospitality. So much so, that I think I'd better hand my car keys to my wife – I wouldn't want to be breathalysed. Here you are, dear...'

The gathering stood in open-mouthed silence as the magistrate handed his wife a set of car keys with an unfurled condom attached. It was almost as if we were watching in slow motion as the unfortunate lady accepted the keys and the other unwanted item before the pair left the room, exchanging glances, apparently unable to speak.

'Cheerio then,' I said brightly, and took my leave as the deputation remained riveted to the spot with shock.

Gerry was waiting for me in the court corridor, drinking from a can of lager, which I took out of his hand and put on the window ledge before taking him outside. 'That's no way to face a crisis,' I said. 'And suppose someone from social services saw you, then it's game set and match, isn't it? You know what they're like.'

'I suppose so, but I've got nothing left to fight with.'

'Well, you just can't give up, that's ridiculous. If that kid means anything to you at all, take my advice – leave the drink alone and start acting like a responsible parent.'

Gerry's eyes moistened, and he turned away as tears streamed down his cheeks. I put an arm around him, and guided him back towards the office.

Three weeks later, I went to court to answer the application for an interim care order. Gerry turned up unshaven, dishevelled, and reeking of alcohol. Scott, his child, wasn't present, and the social services presented the case very strongly in favour of taking the child away. I have to admit I resented their attitude, because they seemed to be treating the case as a personal contest, more concerned about beating us than about the boy's best interests.

But beat us they did. The chairman of the magistrates was from an upper-middle-class background, had sent his own son to public school, and was wealthy enough to retire early and live a good life in one of the more expensive suburbs of Rotherham. He was a fair man and I had no complaints about his judgement, but he had never really been able to see how the other half lived, and was appalled at the catalogue of material the social services had thrown at us. He informed the court that the magistrates had come to the conclusion that an interim care order was in the best interests of the child. Scott would be placed in the care of the local authority at an address designated by them, and after four weeks full information would be placed before the court to see what steps had been taken to improve the situation.

Whilst it was heart-breaking for Gerry, he had left the court with little option. But even though the result was entirely his own fault, I couldn't help feeling sorry for a man whose life had taken such a dramatic turn downward. By the time I got out of court Gerry had gone, and I wandered down to the Cross Keys, where, sure enough, my instinct proved right: there he was, sitting at the bar with a pint of lager and a double brandy.

Back at the office, I was surprised to see Mrs Mott busy polishing my desk: she was usually gone by now. 'You're here late, Mrs Mott,' I said.

'Yes, Mr Smith,' she said. 'I wanted to... I... It's not my fault. I don't know how to tell you this, but...' She looked, and indeed was, very upset, so I asked her to sit down. 'Would you like something to drink?' I asked.

'Oh, that would be very nice.' Astonishingly, before I got the chance to order a cup of tea, she asked for a large whisky. I poured it out and gave it to her, and then she delivered the bombshell.

'I've been to the hospital, Mr Smith, and they've told me I'm not very well "down there". You know, women's problems.'

'Oh dear, I'm sorry to hear that, Mrs Mott,' I said. 'Is there anything I can do?'

'It's not that,' said Mrs Mott. 'You see, it's not... I'm not going to be able to...' She took a gulp of whisky. 'I've got cancer, Mr Smith,' she said. 'I've been poorly for some time, but I thought it was just a bit of old age. But it's not, and the hospital say I've got to have chemotherapy.'

Shocked, I blurted out tactlessly, 'I'm sure they'll be able to rectify the problem.'

Mrs Mott looked at the floor, which was a reply in itself. After a few minutes, while I desperately tried to think of something sensible to say, she said, 'They don't know at home,' she said, 'and I don't know how to tell them. But I'm going to have the treatment just the same. You never know, there may be a chance.'

'There's always a chance, Mrs Mott,' I said, placing my arm around her shoulders. 'When does this treatment start?'

'On Monday,' she said. 'I've got my sister to stand in for me here. She goes on a bit, but she's honest and a good worker. If you'll allow it, she'll take over.'

'Just until you come back,' I said confidently.

'Well, I also have to have an operation, so the doctor seems to think I'll have to retire.'

The subject was clearly upsetting her – and me – so I tried to change it. 'Let's see what happens, Mrs Mott. I think you'll be okay. You look very well to me!' I was lying, because she didn't. If I'd only taken the trouble to look at her more carefully, I would have noticed a deterioration in her complexion and overall demeanour.

'You're good men, you and Mr Wilford, you're both gentlemen. You've been so good to me, I can't bear the thought of letting you down.'

Here was a woman facing the biggest struggle of her life, and all she could think about was letting her employer down. I was almost moved to tears by her thoughtfulness.

'I'll finish tomorrow, then, if I may, and bring Vera in with me to show her the ropes.'

'We'll all come and visit you, Mrs Mott,' I said. 'And I'm sure you'll be okay.'

She smiled, then turned and walked out of the room. 'I know

you'll be okay!' I shouted after her in wilful denial. It had been a bloody awful day, full of bad news and trauma, and there was I, fumbling to reassure a blameless woman whose only fault in life had been to grow old.

The next day when I arrived, a lady whom I estimated to be in her late sixties greeted me at the top of the stairs. She had grey hair combed back into a bun, was just over five feet tall, but fat, and had the same emerald green eyes and pleasant, honest face as her sister. She was wearing a multi-coloured pinafore and a pair of blue fur-rimmed carpet slippers, which she caught me looking at.

'Hello, bunions,' she said, pointing to her feet. 'You'll be Mr Smith. I'm Vera George, Alice Mott's sister. Pleased to meet you.'

We shook hands, and I was amazed by the force of her grip, as Mrs Mott appeared. 'I see you've introduced yourself, Vera.'

'Aye,' said Vera. 'You're right, he's not bad-looking, though he could do with a haircut and losing a bit of weight.'

'Oh God,' I thought, concealing a smile, 'she's just like her sister!'

When Mrs Mott was about to leave, all the staff gathered together so that we could make a presentation; we had bought her a television and video and a large bouquet of flowers. She was overcome by emotion, as were we all – even Wilf had to clear a lump in his throat, and Roy Bennett looked more soldierly than ever, as he always did when he was moved, but felt he ought to keep a stiff upper lip.

It was a moderately uneventful week, and each day I checked with Vera about her sister, to be told that 'no news was good news'. But on Friday of the following week, Vera was less chirpy than usual when I asked, 'How are things, Vera?'

'Not too good. Alice has got to have an operation on Monday. They've decided there's no alternative.'

'Oh no,' I replied. 'What else has the doctor said?'

Vera took her time repeating what she had been told, clearly upset at her sister's plight. 'They don't know if they've caught it in time, but one thing's for sure, if she doesn't have this operation the cancer will spread. They told her that without it she'd only have six months left.'

I shook my head in disbelief. 'I'm sorry to have mentioned it now, Vera. Is there anything I can do?'

'Nothing, thank you, Mr Smith. Or – well, there is one thing,' she said. 'If you could, that is…'

'Just name it, Vera. I'll do whatever I can.'

'It'd be nice if you could pop in to see her before the operation.'

'I'd be delighted to. The only reason I've not visited before is that I know it's only two visitors per person, and I didn't want to get in the way of the family.'

'No, that's all right, Mr Smith, she'd be thrilled to bits to see you.'

'Then I'll go tomorrow lunchtime, after Saturday court, if that's OK?'

'That's smashing,' she said, wiping a tear from her face as she went about her business.

Next day I headed off to the hospital in Sheffield, and on reaching the right ward went to the sister's office to ask if it was all right for me to see Mrs Mott, since it wasn't quite visiting time yet. The sister, a rotund lady with bright red hair, a vivacious smile, and a kind face which lit up when she smiled, told me that I was expected, and took me to a room Mrs Mott shared with five other ladies. She was in a corner by the window, and was pleased to see me, as I was to see her, although by now she looked tired and grey, and as she sat up in bed pain flashed across her emerald eyes like a beacon.

'It seems a silly question, Mrs Mott, but how are you?'

'I'm all right, Mr Smith. I'm in a bit of discomfort, but it's not too bad. It's the waiting, really, gets you down, but I've made some good friends in here. That's Mrs Essex over there, she's got the same problem as me, and the lady at the far end, Mrs Broughton, lives not far from us, so I've got plenty of company, and they're all nice ladies. The boys come twice a day, they're a good set, they really are, and our Vera pops in after work. She's settling down well, she says, having a marvellous time.'

'She's doing very well indeed, we're very happy with her, but there's only one Mrs Mott.'

Her eyes moistened and she placed her hand on mine. 'Thanks ever so much for coming to see me,' she said. 'It's so nice of you.'

'Not at all. I've brought you some Turkish Delight; Vera says it's your favourite. Everyone sends their love, and Wilf's coming tomorrow. He says he's going to bring you a bottle of Guinness.'

'Well, he'll have to sneak it in – they're very strict here about alcohol!'

We both laughed, then a nurse came in and told me she needed to do some tests, so I prepared to leave with some final words of encouragement. 'Don't forget, Mrs Mott, I want you back in that office as soon as you've recovered.'

She smiled and nodded, and I thought what a tremendously brave woman she was.

Wilf went to see Mrs Mott on the Sunday, and I understand he did take her a bottle of Guinness, which she put in her locker as she wasn't allowed to drink it before the operation, but it was the thought that counted. Vera didn't work on the Monday or Tuesday, because she had a great deal of running about to do looking after her family and standing by for calls from the hospital. She rang me on Tuesday morning to tell me that the operation had taken place and early indications were good, but that the effects of the drugs and anaesthetic meant Mrs Mott slept most of the time, so it would be some days before she was fit to receive visitors other than her immediate family.

The next morning the police rang to say that one of my drug-addict clients had committed suicide whilst on remand at the prison. And there was Mrs Mott in hospital, fighting for her life. Somehow it just didn't seem fair.

SEVENTEEN

GERRY'S KID, AND I DISCOVER CRUISING

The next few weeks saw a remarkable change in Gerry Woodward's attitude. Whilst he had not completely given up alcohol, he had cut down to less than a third of his previous intake, smartened himself up, signed on at the local technical college for a retraining course in computers, which he was attending each weekday, and was seeing his son regularly at the foster home. He had worked hard, without any outside assistance, and our campaign for the return of his son was gathering momentum. The case had been adjourned for a full formal hearing, which meant that all manner of reports would be prepared by social workers, in which the interests of the child were quite properly paramount.

One of our main problems was Miss Stackpole, the social worker assigned to the case. A spinster of about fifty, reputed to have considerable experience in dealing with children, she was the epitome of the left-wing assertive female, a formidable woman of heavy build, with a short, severe hairstyle, apart from one tuft of hair on the crown of her head, which resisted any attempt to flatten it. She wore sturdy walking shoes and a tweed suit enhanced by a string of dress pearls, and had a habit of peering distrustfully over her half-moon spectacles. Unfortunately Gerry's relationship with her had got off on the wrong foot, so Miss Stackpole had already formed a dislike of him, but he was doing his best.

I had had grave concerns myself, prior to Gerry's rehabilitation, but had become more optimistic as his attitude and conduct improved. The catalyst for this was one upsetting visit when I had gone along to check Scott was being properly cared for. He was with a very nice family who had fostered many children in the past, which had given them a considerable insight into the plight of young people caught up in such difficulties, so they were sympathetic to Gerry's point of view.

Scott was sitting watching television when Gerry and I turned up, and we were shown every courtesy, although the family were midway through preparing the evening meal and could no doubt well have done without us. I left Gerry with his son for ten minutes or so while I talked to the foster parents, and when we all returned to the lounge we saw Gerry and Scott hugging each other, both in tears. We heard Gerry promise Scott that he would get him home, which seemed the only way he could be placated, and I was pleased that the foster parents had witnessed this, for such outbursts of emotion cannot be orchestrated, and the incident could become a useful part of my case.

Another of Gerry's difficulties had been housing, but one day he came into the office bubbling over with excitement, to report that he had acquired a small terraced house in a suburb of Rotherham. There was a tiny garden area at the front, a larger one with a shed at the rear, and although the house needed decorating it was wind- and watertight. Over the next two or three weeks, Gerry used every hour and penny he had on the substantial task of turning the house into a home. He invited me to make a conducted tour when he finished decorating, and I was truly impressed.

The following day I telephoned social services to tell Miss Stackpole about Gerry's efforts in his new house, and suggested that she should see it for herself. Her curt reply made it clear that this was a conversation she did not want to have. 'I'll see it in due course, and it will form part of my report. But it is a little late in the day and, I suspect, has been done for the purpose of the case.'

'Well, of course it's for the purpose of the case! That's the whole idea, isn't it? He was given that time to show what he could do to provide a home for the child.'

'I'll be the judge of that,' said Miss Stackpole with a studied lack of interest, 'and I will take into account such matters as I think appropriate.'

Conscious that my temper was rising, I decided she was antagonistic enough without my making matters worse by having a blazing row with her, so left it at that. In a way I was annoyed with myself for not taking her to task, but what would that have achieved? One of the difficulties in my profession is that sometimes when you are in the right you cannot say so for fear of offending someone who holds sanction over your case, which is why so many lawyers are called two-faced. Sometimes they have to be.

My brooding was interrupted by Vera. 'Want a cup of tea, duck?'

'Yes please, Vera, two sugars.'

'You shouldn't be having sugar, you should have Canderel, it's much better for you. Too much sugar can lead to wind. It always gets me like that if I have a lot of sweet stuff. Anyway, I've brought you a piece of carrot cake I baked yesterday.'

'Oh, lovely,' I said. I don't like carrot cake, but she was watching so I felt obliged to eat it to avoid giving offence. It was tasteless apart from a slight hint of carrot, and it simply confirmed that this was the vegetable I hated most.

The telephone rang, and Tracy informed me that Brenda Dobkin was in reception for her appointment.

Big Brenda Dobkin feared no one. Her muscular arms led to hands which were about the size of a garden spade; she was very manly, and her forte in life was arm-wrestling. Given that there wasn't a woman in Rotherham to beat her, she concentrated on the men. Every time I met her in town she had her Rottweiler/Alsatian cross Tiger with her, the most easy-going beast I'd ever seen. So it was a great surprise to me that Brenda was clutching a summons under the Dogs Act, applying to the court for an order that she keep Tiger under control.

'It was that bloody postman,' Brenda said. 'Tiger hates postmen. Whenever he sees one he goes barmy. I've told thee before.'

'Yes, I remember you telling me some weeks ago. Is that what happened here?'

'Aye. The postman came down the drive and Tiger was out. He just went for 'im. Whenever he sees that uniform he goes barmy.'

I looked at the summons and accompanying papers, and it seemed that Tiger had bitten a postman on the left buttock. The police had the power to bring a summons either to apply for an animal to be destroyed, or for an order that it should be kept under control – which is rather like a suspended sentence for the dog; if he does it again the police have the right to request its destruction.

'Well, don't worry too much, Brenda, because they're not asking that Tiger be destroyed, just that you keep him under proper control.' I explained the ramifications of such an order, which seemed to appease her somewhat.

'Will tha go to court with me?' she asked.

'Of course I will,' I replied reluctantly, knowing that legal aid wasn't available for this sort of case.

'Will Tiger 'ave to go?'

'No,' I replied. 'I don't think he'd understand what they were saying to him anyway.'

Brenda forced a courteous laugh. 'Nay, I don't suppose he would,' she agreed, and went away reasonably happy.

The following week, I sweated over Gerry Woodward's court papers. The social services had prepared a written statement for the court, which came down very heavily in favour of a care order. Miss Stackpole had made her decision without taking into account Gerry's recent efforts, which she dismissed as being carried out just to impress the court, without any real possibility of being sustained.

The hearing took place in Court Number 3, and while I represented Gerry Woodward, social services were represented by a council solicitor supported by Miss Stackpole and her assistant, plus three other members of staff. They must have cleaned out their entire offices of personnel just for one case! Our supporters' bench of just Gerry and me looked painfully inadequate, but then we couldn't compete with the finances at the council's disposal.

Miss Stackpole opened the case, surely the most aggressive case I had ever heard, including such scathing, one-sided attacks on Gerry and his circumstances that I almost lost my temper. All morning she threw every bag of manure in the armoury, and left me thinking she had a personal vendetta against us. But Gerry gave as good as he got in the witness box, much to Miss Stackpole's annoyance; he admitted his drink problems and, even more astonishingly, accepted he hadn't fully recovered. He came over as a man more worthy of sympathy than anything else, but despite our attempts to show what improvements he'd made in his lifestyle, the court were suspicious. In an endeavour to dispel their fears I pointed out that his honesty with the court deserved great credit, and showed he was not willing to fudge his responsibilities.

I thought I had done enough to avoid the care order and let Scott go home, even if he had to be subject to a supervision order, which would still mean a lot of involvement with social services, but the magistrates thought differently. Scott was taken away from Gerry as they made a care order. I found this decision hard to accept, because I had allowed sentiment to creep in. I'll never forget the sight of Scott being led away from the court, almost like a criminal but without a conviction.

We would be able to bring our own proceedings after three months, if we could show that altered circumstances should prompt the court to reconsider the case. I decided that we would try again, provided that Gerry could stay away from the bottle, and he was determined to.

Miss Stackpole was delighted with the result, and preened

herself on her victory. Well she might have won the battle, but she wasn't going to win the war if I had anything to do with it.

Unfortunately, I hadn't. Some two months later, as I ran the gauntlet of the local winos who spent their day lounging around the benches in the churchyard on my way to the office, I noticed one member of the group was more familiar than the rest. It was Gerry Woodward.

It was September 1987 and I had never worked harder in my life, but I was enjoying my work and such trappings of success as it brought. We were becoming well known locally, which meant we attracted a fair amount of work, but also an abundance of raffle tickets from contacts who thought that we were fair game for sales. One of these was quite expensive, with tickets at ten pounds each, but the star prize was a car, and the second prize a cruise on the famous P&O shipping line, travelling to such exotic places as Greece, Egypt and Israel.

I had quite forgotten about my ticket, including the fact that the grand draw was to take place at a gala dinner at a large hotel in Sheffield to which I hadn't been invited, and in any case the tickets for that were a whopping £50 each. I was sitting in my office preparing to go to court when Sheila brought in my post. Amongst the usual bills and demands for cigarettes or Red Cross parcels from Armley jail, one letter caught my eye. It was from the charity responsible for the raffle, and I couldn't believe its contents – I had won second prize! The fortnight's cruise for two which would include visits to the Acropolis in Athens, Haifa in Israel for a trip to Bethlehem and Jerusalem, but best of all, Alexandria in Egypt, to see the Sphinx and pyramids at Giza, and the fabulous Tutankhamun mask in Cairo Museum.

When the time came, Jennifer and I left Rebecca with her grandparents, flew to Athens, and boarded the ship in the famous Piraeus harbour. After finding our way to our cabin, we joined most of the travellers on deck to wave at scores of uninterested Greeks as the ship left harbour to the strains of 'We Are Sailing' from a slightly out-of-tune band. A bald gentleman with a young face was standing next to me, and we struck up a conversation, discussing the various ports of call, and agreed to share a drink if we should bump into each other later that evening. Then, after completing a tour of the ship, Jennifer and I returned to our cabin to be reunited with our luggage.

On a cruise all the events of the day are mapped out in a day sheet, giving you the various options you might be interested in, and someone suggested that it was rather like Butlin's. However, with all respect to Butlin's, cruising is vastly different. My favourite on-board activities were the meals, which were always a grand affair, particularly the seven-course dinners; alternate nights were formal, when the dress code was black tie. At pre-dinner drinks in the various bars the ladies showed off their latest designer wear, scrutinising each new arrival and discussing the likely value of her dress.

The first evening was a formal night, and we all trooped rather nervously into the dining room as the dinner gong sounded, to be welcomed by an array of smartly dressed waiters offering plastic smiles, with an eye on the tips at the end of the cruise. (Admittedly the service was superb, more than living up to the quality of the food and the extensive wine cellar – which could only have been appreciated by a true connoisseur with very deep pockets, so I resisted the temptation to break fresh ground and stuck to the house red.) Luckily we had been allocated to share a table with David and Linda Selley from Chesterfield, who both worked in their family's textile import/export business. They were really good company, quick to enjoy a good laugh, so we got on very well.

The next day Jennifer disappeared into the spa, and I went to the morning lecture explaining the organised trip to Bethlehem and Jerusalem; aided by a selection of slides and videos, the speaker gave us a potted version of the history of the area, and a useful list of do's and don'ts. At lunchtime, since Jennifer still hadn't reappeared, I repaired to the top-deck open-air restaurant, to peruse one of the most extensive wine lists I'd seen in a long time. Waiting to place my order, I became aware of a familiar presence – my bald acquaintance from the sailing, bedecked in a multi-coloured T-shirt, Bermuda shorts and sandals, with a smudge of suntan cream on his already reddening pate – the archetypal Englishman abroad.

At that point a steward walked past with a large sheet of Perspex, which acted as a mirror. I saw myself, bedecked in striped Bermuda shorts and a multicoloured T-shirt. Another Englishman abroad, I thought, and a fair cop.

My acquaintance and I exchanged nods as we were being served with our T-bone steaks. Then he opened the conversation. 'You like steak, then?' he said.

Quick as a flash, I replied, 'No, I'm a vegetarian, this is for the dog.'

We both laughed, and went on to share a table. When our respective spouses eventually joined us we enjoyed a sumptuous meal together, and achieved an instant rapport. The man introduced himself as Malcolm Garton, who lived in Hull with his wife Barbara and daughter Andrea, and we enjoyed some good banter, including a competition to guess each other's profession.

My first guess was that he was a chef, because he obviously relished his food, but then I decided on some form of sales representative. He was equally at sea about me, and when I told him I was a solicitor he said, 'But solicitors are generally reserved, cultured and smart.' Then he put me out of my misery by telling me he was an undertaker.

It wasn't long before Malcolm and I were swapping anecdotes about our respective professions, and the four of us agreed to dine together that night, meeting in one of the lounges. I was ready early, so I left Jennifer dressing and took a stroll around the deck, where I watched the sunset from the stern – a magnificent sight, its reflection dancing from wave to wave as the ship glided serenely through the calm sea, and the steel band played with commendable empathy. The atmosphere on board was equally magnificent, people walking the decks with their pre-dinner cocktails, resplendent in their elegant evening clothes. I leant on the rail and looked out to sea, feeling warm and contented. 'James Bond would do this,' I thought. 'White tux, carnation, and…'

I was interrupted by a friendly waiter, who offered to fetch me a drink. 'Vodka martini, please,' I said, playing out the role for my own amusement. 'Shaken, not stirred.'

The time had come to meet the Gartons. As I finished my drink and turned to go, a bald, fat and rather squat American, wearing a white tux, appeared at the rail. 'Makes you feel like James Bond,' he drawled in a Southern accent.

'Yes, I suppose it does,' I replied.

'Yes, sir, it sure does. Yee hah!' he shouted. Every time I saw him after that he called me Mr Bond, so I called him Davy Crockett, which he took as a great compliment.

We enjoyed the usual superb dinner with the Gartons, with the sweet forming the grand finale, when the lights were dimmed and, at a drum roll, the waiters marched in with flaming crêpes Suzette. Afterwards we retired to the lounge for coffee and liqueurs and watched the cabaret.

At midnight the party broke up, and the Gartons and Jennifer went off to bed, but I still wasn't sleepy, so I thought I'd have a look at the casino, which was in the piano bar at the stern of the ship. The pianist was playing suitable background music for the fly-boys of the cruise to show off their Armani suits, Rolex watches and large wads of £20 notes: I had a Marks and Spencer dinner suit, Seiko watch, and three crisp new fivers – but I was prepared to blow all three! I bought five pounds' worth of chips and stood at the roulette table as though I knew what I was doing, but I couldn't play for two reasons:

1. I couldn't get a place; and
2. I didn't know how.

Nonetheless, I tried to look as though I did, and as I stood casually in the queue a man with dark, swarthy features leaned towards me conspiratorially, as if about to impart a great secret.

'Do you think you'll win, then?' I asked naively.

'Probably,' said Omar Sharif. 'You see, you need to remember three things: feel the game; see the pea; and watch the croupier. Got it?' he said mysteriously.

'Yes,' I said, though really I hadn't got a clue.

Within minutes Omar had made his mark: twenty pounds on number 26. 'No more bets, *mesdames et messieurs*,' said 'Henri' with a false French accent (I found out later his real name was Henry Parsons and he was from Mablethorpe). 'Number 26!'

I couldn't believe it. Surely it was just luck? I watched even more closely as he put fifty pounds on number 36. 'No more bets, *mesdames et messieurs...*'

Omar winked at me as number 36 came up. 'I'm tired,' he said. 'I go to my bed,' and off he went with about £3,000 of P&O's money.

His place was left empty, and I found myself a somewhat reluctant occupant of his seat. I tried to look casual as possible, giving a knowing nod and nonchalant smile to the other players as they waited eagerly for the next game. Hands moved across the table with considerable speed, and I couldn't see how to apply Omar's instructions, so I proceeded to put five pounds on number 13.

'No more bets, *mesdames et messieurs*, no more bets please... Number 4.'

'Oh bollocks,' I thought, as I tried to laugh off the cost of the equivalent of six pints of duty-free lager, and decided I'd better follow Mr Sharif's other principle, and go to bed.

EIGHTEEN

JACK'S CAR BOOT

One beautiful autumn morning, a few days after our return from the cruise, I arrived at the office to find waiting in reception one Ronald Arthur Mulligan, generally known as Dimsy for his intellectual attainment. He was truly thick, but his sunny disposition made him quite likeable. Unfortunately he was a persistent but unsuccessful thief, and had been charged with stealing a hundred metres of barbed wire, which had once formed a fence around a building site to protect it from thieves... The fencing found its way into Ronnie's back yard and, unfortunately for him, so did the police. They identified the stolen property easily, because it still had the contractor's logo fixed at intervals along the wire, with the words: 'Keep Out. Trespassers Will Be Prosecuted.'

Ronnie greeted me with a wide grin, shaking my hand firmly. He was a large chap, just over six foot and around sixteen stone, with the air of a nightclub bouncer, and his drawl added a touch of comedy to his persona. We went into an interview room where he handed me his charge sheets, the back of which appeared to have been marinated in tomato sauce. I opened the paperwork delicately, then read the narrative of the charge.

'Are you pleading guilty to this, Ronnie?' I asked.

'Well...' said Ronnie, even more slowly than usual, 'The... coppers... found it in... my yard.'

'Yes, so you'll be pleading guilty then?' I asked.

'When... they... found... it... in... my... yard... they... took...

it... back... to... the... police station.'

'Yes, I realise that. So it looks like it's a guilty plea then, Ronnie?'

'I... can't... really... Well... what... can... I... say? I'm...'

'Stupid?' I thought. 'Guilty!' I said in a raised voice.

'Well... yes.'

'Thank God for that. I thought you were never going to say it. It's all right, Ronnie, I understand entirely. The police found it in your yard, so there can be no doubt about your guilt. Is that right?'

'Well... they... found... it... in... my... yard...'

Before he could finish, I wrote 'Guilty' down on my instructions sheet. To save time, I framed my questions so the logical answer would have to be 'yes' or 'no', cutting down the interview from an hour to just twenty minutes. Finally I gave Ronnie the legal aid papers to sign, which he did with great difficulty. He was due at court the following Monday, so I explained the procedure.

'I want you at court at a quarter to ten in the morning. You be there with your best suit on, and I'll see what we can do for you.'

Ronnie looked perplexed. 'I... haven't... got... a suit,' he said.

'Well, can you put a collar and tie on? A clean white shirt as well,' I added, suddenly having a horrible vision of him turning up with just a collar and tie but no shirt. Ronnie looked at me blankly. 'Well, anything, then. Come as you are, if it's a problem.' Although to be fair, a Mickey Mouse T-shirt with the legend 'Don't f*** with Mickey' and striped jogging bottoms would not necessarily gain him great favour.

'I... can't... go... like... this,' said Ronnie. 'They'll... think... I'm an... idiot.'

'Get away,' I replied sarcastically. 'Well, just turn up, anyway.'

On the Monday I was pleased to see Ronnie had turned up bright and early, but wearing a curious grey suit with a cutaway-style jacket, and the initials RM on the lapel. 'What... do... you... think... of... this... suit?' he asked.

'It looks very smart, Ron, and it's an excellent fit, although the sleeves look a little short.' In fact they only reached down to his elbows.

'That's... the... new... look. It's... got... my... initials... on it ... as well,' said Ronnie, pointing at the lapel. 'Look... RM... Ronnie... Mulligan.'

At that point the usher wheezed me into court, where Ronnie's case was the first on, and I set about mitigating his misdemeanours to the magistrates. The chairperson was a courteous lady in her sixties, which made her popular with the defence solicitors, but she was a tough sentencer, and wasn't impressed by Ronnie's list of previous convictions. She told us that the magistrates were considering a custodial sentence, so the case would be adjourned for the preparation of a probation report. Ronnie missed the point entirely, and when the case was adjourned for four weeks he thought he'd got off scot-free.

The next day, when one of my cases was called on in Court Number 2, I looked at the defendant and couldn't help noticing that he too was wearing a grey suit, cut away at the waist, with half-length sleeves and the initials RM embroidered in red on the lapel – a duplicate of the one Ronnie had worn the day before. I looked at the court list to check his name, which was Adrian Fenton, so obviously his initials weren't RM. Intrigued, I was tempted to ask him where he'd got the suit, but as he was a lot bigger than me, I decided to put it down to coincidence.

On Wednesday, I was interviewing clients in my office when in walked a local ne'er-do-well called Eric Parker, a dab hand at removing stereos from motor vehicles by fixing their alarms so that they wouldn't go off until he had completed the theft. As he sat in the interview chair, the first thing I noticed was that he was wearing a grey suit with a cutaway waist and short sleeves, which on closer scrutiny revealed the letters RM in red on the lapel.

We talked about his case, but my attention was continually drawn to his clothing, and at one point Eric expostulated, 'Are tha listenin' to me or what? That's the third time tha's asked me that!'

'I'm sorry, Eric, I was a little distracted. In fact, I was wondering about your suit.'

'Me suit? What's wrong wi' it?'

'Nothing. It's very smart, in fact, though I don't quite understand why the sleeves are so short.'

'It's the new style, innit? Short sleeves and the cutaway waist.' The cutaway waist hadn't really worked on Eric, whose forty-four-inch waist supported a huge beer belly.

My curiosity got the better of me, and I had to ask, 'What do the initials RM mean?'

'Oh,' said Eric, 'that's Ricardo Monchetti. The maker, innit? It's Italian, the new style, cutaway waist and short sleeves, and that's a designer label. It's the latest import. It's going to be all the rage an' pull the birds.'

It seemed to me that whatever Eric wore wouldn't help him 'pull the birds', for he was fat and bald and toothless, and the armpits of his jacket were stained with sweat. 'Where did you get it, Eric, if you don't mind me asking?'

'Why, does tha want one?'

'Er, not really,' I said. 'I'm not too keen on the sleeves or the cutaway jacket.'

'What's up wi' thee? It's the latest fashion, this. I got it from a mate of mine, he's importing 'em from Italy. Tha wants to go out to our club tonight, all them as is available will be wearing these.'

'What do you mean, available?' I asked.

'Well, what you do, you put one of these Ricardo Monchetti suits on and that tells the birds you're available, like. So they come and chat you up, 'cos it's like a call sign which shouts out to 'em, "I'm 'ere if tha wants me, baby!" '

Something told me that Eric had been had. 'Which mate did you say?' I asked.

'Jack Heptonstall got it for me. 'E's got one or two from one of his pals in Italy.'

'Ah,' I replied thoughtfully. So Jack had acquired a load of suits from goodness knows where and was flogging them all around Rotherham. I completed my instructions and Eric went on his way, doubtless to the local working men's club in the hope that all the local 'birds' would drape themselves around him.

The following day I had a full list of appointments, including Ronnie Mulligan, who was coming in to go through his papers. I was just saying farewell to a lady who'd been charged with having no television licence when I heard a commotion in reception: the sound of a dog barking and growling. I went in to see what was happening, and there in one corner, being restrained by Big Brenda, was Tiger, whilst in the opposite corner, trembling with fear, was Ronnie Mulligan.

'Tell 'im to sod off,' said Brenda.

'Sod off, Ronnie,' I said, and Ronnie sought sanctuary in the corridor, whereupon Tiger immediately sat down and calmly wagged his tail. It was a bizarre incident, because usually Tiger only bothered with postmen...

At that moment, things began to fit, and I suppose if I'd been brighter I would have seen it earlier. The jackets cut away at the waist, with those half-length sleeves... The dog always went for postmen, but never for anyone else... The initials on the lapel – RM, Ricardo Monchetti... and what else might RM stand for, apart from Ronnie Mulligan? Jack Heptonstall was the key, and I resolved to see him, if only to satisfy my own curiosity.

That Sunday I had to go to Worksop to see a witness. Having taken the statement I needed, I was driving back to Rotherham when I saw a sign for Thorsby market, a very large car-boot sale where all manner of items are sold, so I decided to look for some bedding plants for my garden. I wandered around until I found a plant stall. Then, armed with a cardboard box full of mixed half-hardy annuals, I was setting off back to the car when I saw on a stall in the distance a large placard announcing 'Ricardo Monchetti designer suits'.

I walked over there. The stall was surrounded by young men trying on suits with short sleeves, cutaway waists and the letters RM on the lapel, and in their midst were Ricardo Monchetti's main British agents, Jack and Albert Heptonstall! Jack even had a tapemeasure hung around his neck, the personification of tailoring excellence.

As usual, Jack's eyes were everywhere. Seeing me, he waved me over with great enthusiasm. 'Now then, Steve, 'ow are you?'

'Well, Jack, and you?'

'Oh, not too bad,' said Jack. 'Just tryin' to get a bit of 'onest work done.'

I looked around the stall. As well as the metal clothes-racks of 'Ricardo Monchetti' suits, there was a large consignment of boxer shorts with no fly, advertised by a sign which read, 'New look from Brazil, as worn by eunuchs in the rain forests, for complete comfort.' Jack gave me four pairs as a present, including one which bore the motif 'What an arse'. He said he'd bought them as seconds from a bankrupt stock supplier, and he proudly showed me all manner of *objets d'art*, such as an old typewriter, an exhaust for an MGB, and a set of vicar's robes.

'The jackets are interesting, Jack,' I said.

'Aye, they are. Italian designer label, Ricardo Monchetti.'

'Really? What's the real truth, Jack? They aren't pinched, are they?'

'Definitely not!' said Jack indignantly. 'I only deal in straight gear. Mebbe they're not really Italian, but the stock supervisor's been there for 'is 'olidays. They were a good buy. I'm knocking 'em out at fifty quid a throw and the lads are buying all I've got.'

'Ricardo Monchetti wouldn't happen to be Italian for Royal Mail, would it?' I asked.

Jack looked at me with mock surprise, as did Albert, who had joined the end of the conversation, then in slow motion the Heptonstall smile broke out on both faces. It turned into a snigger, and in no time all three of us were laughing raucously. When he could speak again, Jack admitted that the jackets were seconds – and in some cases, I'd have thought, thirds – owing to various design faults. But with optimism and some forward-thinking, Jack and Albert had turned then into the designer wear of the year for the Rotherham area. Yet I somehow thought I'd never be able to look at a postman in the same light again.

The next day I parked near the office, and met Big Brenda walking the opposite way. We passed the time of day, and Tiger covered my trousers with drool. As I walked on I heard Tiger barking ferociously, and turned to see Brenda pulling him away from my car – with some difficulty, despite her considerable strength. Then I realised it was probably because I had a Ricardo Monchetti jacket on a coat-hanger in the back of my car, covering up the eunuchs' underwear and vicar's robes I'd bought for Pagey!

In the office, I was surprised to find Mrs Mott sitting in reception.

'Hello,' I said. 'It's great to see you, but should you be here? How are you?'

'I wanted to tell you myself, Mr Smith...' she began, and my heart sank. But only for a moment, because she went on, 'I've got the all-clear for the moment. I'm on three-monthly checks, but so far it's looking good. How's my sister doing?'

'She's great, but we'd rather have you – if you're able... ?' I said tentatively.

'I will be in three months, they reckon,' said Mrs Mott. 'In the meanwhile I just came to say thanks.' She squeezed my hand and smiled, then presented me with a lovely silk tie. 'For being such a support,' she said, and left.

For once, I exulted – one of the good guys had won! Although our overheads and commitments were growing, and the banks' ever-growing risk-aversion threatened the future of our firm as our overdraft mushroomed, one human's life had changed for the better.

I was suddenly very happy, too, that the Heptonstalls were back in our midst, for they added to the gaiety of a life that held more than its share of depressing and even tragic moments. If only I knew what trouble they had in store for me next...